Meaningful Making:

Projects and Inspirations for Fab Labs + Makerspaces

Meaningful Making:

Projects and Inspirations for Fab Labs + Makerspaces

Edited by Paulo Blikstein, Sylvia Libow Martinez, and Heather Allen Pang

CONSTRUCTING MODERN KNOWLEDGE PRESS

All marks are the property of their respective owners.

All photos are credited to the article author unless otherwise noted.

Constructing Modern Knowledge Press

Torrance, CA USA

cmkpress.com

Print book ISBN: 978-0-9891511-9-1

e-book ISBN: 978-0-9891511-2-2

EDU039000 EDUCATION / Computers & Technology

EDU029030 EDUCATION / Teaching Methods & Materials / Science & Technology

Cover design by Chad McCallum

Interior design and production by SunDried Penguin

Edited by Dorothy M. Taguchi, The Linguistic Edge

Contents

About the FabLearn Fellows Initiative

The FabLearn Fellows program was created by Paulo Blikstein's Transformative Learning Technologies Laboratory (TLTL), an academic research group within Stanford University's Graduate School of Education. The Fellows program brings together experienced educators from all over the world to contribute to research about the "makers" culture and digital fabrication in education and to create an open-source library of curriculum. The 2014–2015 FabLearn Fellows cohort is composed of a diverse group of eighteen educators and makers. The Fellows represent six countries, including eight states in the United States, and work with students from a wide variety of demographics at public and independent schools, community organizations, museums, and nonprofits.

The FabLearn Fellows program was created as part of a larger project sponsored by the National Science Foundation entitled "Infusing Learning Sciences Research into Digital Fabrication in Education and the Makers' Movement" (NSF Award 1349163, Division of Information & Intelligent Systems).

FabLearn Fellow Goals

Despite the recent popularity of the maker movement and fabrication labs in education, most teachers work in isolation, cut off from other practitioners doing similar projects as well as learning sciences researchers. One of the main objectives of the FabLearn Fellows program is to bring researchers and practitioners together to help bridge these gaps, learn from each other's experiences, share these lessons with their local community, and together create educational materials for the rest of the teaching community.

Through this project, we hope to answer three major questions:

- How can we generate an open-source set of constructionist curricular materials well adapted for makerspaces and fabrication labs in educational settings?
- How are teachers adapting their own curriculum in face of these new "making" technologies, and how can they be better supported? What challenges do teachers face when trying to adopt project-based, constructionist, digital fabrication activities in their classrooms and after-school programs?
- How are schools approaching teacher development, parental/community involvement, and issues around traditional assessment?

About the FabLearn Labs

FabLearn Labs (formerly known as FabLab@ School labs) are physical makerspaces in K–12 schools developed by TLTL and managed in collaboration with US and international partners. While today there are a growing number of fabrication labs in school settings, in 2009 FabLab@School was the first such program designed from the ground up specifically to serve grades 6–12.

There are currently FabLearn Lab installations on the Stanford University campus (California), and in Moscow (Russia), Bangkok (Thailand), Palo Alto (California), Barcelona (Spain), Melbourne (Australia), Guadalajara (Mexico), and Aarhus (Denmark). Additional installations are planned for East Palo Alto (California), Brazil, Finland, and Poland in 2016.

The intellectual roots of FabLearn Labs (and much of the other work within TLTL) extend back to the work of Seymour Papert, a pioneer in the field of educational technologies, and his collaborators at the MIT Media Lab. Papert and his colleagues developed Logo, a programming language designed for children and the first systems for educational robotics. Papert's constructionist perspective (a belief that children learn most effectively when they build artifacts and share with peers) is at the heart of the FabLearn Labs program.

The original Fab Lab was conceived in the early 2000s in the Media Lab at MIT by Neil Gershenfeld (with collaboration of Bakhtiar Mitkak) as a creative space for university students. Within five years the concept had been transplanted successfully to community centers and entrepreneurial centers around the globe under the banner of the Fab Foundation. In this book, the spaces that are affiliated with the Fab Foundation are called Fab Labs, while those not associated are called fab labs, fablabs, makerspaces, or their own unique name based on the preference of the organization and author.

Paulo Blikstein, who began researching digital fabrication in education in 2004 as part of his doctoral work, created the FabLearn Lab concept when he joined the Stanford faculty in 2008, and designed the first-ever digital fabrication lab at a school of education.

About this book

This book is a compilation of some of the work of the 2014–2015 cohort of FabLearn Fellows. Included are articles about making and fabrication in many different learning spaces, ideas for projects, reflections, assessment strategies, and much more. Many of the articles and projects include resources for additional reading and exploration, and every FabLearn Fellow has a page on the FabLearn website (fablearn.stanford.edu/fellows/fellows) where more projects, details, and contact information can be found.

Acknowledgements

Contributing FabLearn Fellow Authors:
Jaymes Dec, Gilson Domingues, Christa Flores, Susan Klimczak, David Malpica, Heather Allen Pang, Roy Ombatti, Keith Ostfeld, Erin Riley, Tracy Rudzitis, Mark Schreiber, Susanna Tesconi, Nalin Tutiyaphuengprasert, Aaron Vanderwerff, and Juliet Wanyiri.

Editors: Paulo Blikstein, Sylvia Libow Martinez, and Heather Allen Pang

Editorial guidance and section introductions:
Sylvia Libow Martinez

FabLearn Fellows project principal investigator:
Dr. Paulo Blikstein, assistant professor at the Stanford University Graduate School of Education and (by courtesy) the Computer Science Department, and director of the Transformative Learning Technologies Lab.

FabLearn Fellows program mentor:
Sylvia Libow Martinez, coauthor of *Invent to Learn: Making, Tinkering, and Engineering in the Classroom,* and president, Constructing Modern Knowledge.

Special thanks:
Diana Garcia (TLTL executive director); Claire Rosenbaum (TLTL senior program manager); Brogan Miller; Janet Kolodner and Christopher Hoadley (NSF program managers); Alicja Żenczykowska; and the students and postdocs at the TLTL.

Transformative Learning Technologies Laboratory

The Transformative Learning Technologies Laboratory (TLTL) is a multidisciplinary group designing and researching new technologies for project-based STEM education. Within the realm of digital fabrication in schools, the TLTL conducts research and disseminates findings through three main programs: FabLearn Labs (educational makerspaces in K–12 schools developed in collaboration with US and international partners, formerly known as the FabLab@School project), the FabLearn Conferences, and the FabLearn Fellows program.

Constructing Modern Knowledge Press

Constructing Modern Knowledge (CMK) Press is a publishing company dedicated to producing books supporting modern learner-centered approaches to education.

Caution

Some of these projects call for tools and materials that can be dangerous if used improperly. Always follow manufacturer's guidelines, safety rules, and use common sense.

Meet the Contributing 2014–2015 FabLearn Fellows

Jaymes Dec

Jaymes Dec is the Fab Lab coordinator at the Marymount School of New York in New York City, United States, an all-girls independent school serving students in pre-K through high school. Dec, who has taught makers of all grade levels from kindergarten to graduate school, currently works primarily with middle school students. In addition to his compulsory technology course, which covers programming, design, and fabrication, he supports teachers in other grades who are integrating design elements into their curriculum. The Marymount School program is a member of MIT's Fab Lab network. In 2013, Dec, concerned that Fab Labs and makerspaces were disproportionately the domain of wealthy schools, cofounded the NYC Makery, a public makerspace for children and families. Dec is the president of the Nerdy Derby, a "no rules" model-car building and racing competition. He is a graduate of the Interactive Telecommunications Program at New York University. He recently joined the faculty at Columbia University's Teachers College.

Gilson Domingues

Gilson Domingues is currently a designer and professor at Anhembi Morumbi University in São Paulo, Brazil, where he teaches game design and digital design. He has also taught in middle school and high school settings. He has extensive experience integrating rapid prototyping and design methods and tools into educational settings. Domingues holds bachelor's and master's degrees in visual arts.

Christa Flores

Christa Flores is a science facilitator and the makerspace coordinator at Hillbrook School in Los Gatos, California, United States. The independent preK–8 school was founded on the principles of constructionism more than eighty years ago and offers a full array of courses in woodshop, ceramics, painting, and robotics. In addition to working with students ages eight to fourteen, Flores teaches fifth-grade problem-based science in a makerspace, with an emphasis on material science, design thinking, and collaborative work. She founded the school's STEAM-centered makerspace in 2012. Flores holds a bachelor's degree in biological anthropology from the University of California, San Diego, and a master's degree in secondary science education from Columbia University's Teachers College.

Susan Klimczak

Susan Klimczak is an education organizer at the South End Technology Center @ Tent City's Learn 2 Teach, Teach 2 Learn program in Boston, Massachusetts, United States. Each year, the institution's three-dozen teenage teachers learn, build, and teach six different technology modules. Together they reach more than eight hundred children at more than twenty-five Boston community organizations through a series of summer camps. Fab Lab 001, the first Fab Lab outside of the MIT Center for Bits and Atoms, is located at the Center. Klimczak has also done academic research for the Ford Foundation, National Science Foundation, and the MIT Media Lab, among others. She is a research affiliate with the MIT Media Lab Lifelong Kindergarten Group. She holds a master's degree in education from Harvard University, a master's in environmental education from Lesley University, and a bachelor of science in electrical engineering from University of Maryland College Park.

David Malpica

David Malpica is the director of FabLab@BCS, at Bullis Charter School, a public K–8 school in Los Altos, California, United States. Malpica works primarily with students from fifth to seventh grades and also collaborates with colleagues on interdisciplinary projects.

Roy Ombatti

Roy Ombatti is the cofounder of Fab Lab Robotics Outreach Program in Nairobi, Kenya, which teaches constructionism and making to children, primarily those from low-income households. He is also the founder and CEO of a hardware start-up in Nairobi, African Born 3D Printing (AB3D). AB3D is a social enterprise dedicated to the local production of affordable 3D printers and 3D printing filament from recycled materials. Through partnerships with other local institutions, Ombatti is setting up 3D printers in schools and developing makerspaces around them. He holds a bachelor's degree in mechanical engineering from the University of Nairobi. During his time at the university, he worked on various projects at the Nairobi Fab Lab.

Keith Ostfeld

Keith Ostfeld is the director of educational technology and exhibit development at the Children's Museum of Houston (CMH), in Houston, Texas, United States. For more than thirty-five years, CMH has focused on educating children ages zero to twelve and their parents and caregivers. The museum partners with many schools and after-school organizations to provide hands-on activities as well as bringing students to the museum's Maker Annex. For the past three years, via his alter ego "Mr. O," Ostfeld has produced more than one hundred "O Wow Moment" STEM-related videos available through the CMH blog.

Heather Allen Pang

Heather Allen Pang teaches history to eighth graders at Castilleja School, a grade 6–12 private school in Palo Alto, California, United States. She herself is a graduate of the all-girls school (class of 1984) and also serves as the school archivist. Castilleja's Bourn Idea Lab is very closely associated with Stanford University's Transformative Learning Technology Lab. Before joining the faculty at Castilleja, Pang taught at the University of California, Davis; Santa Rosa Junior College; and American River College. She holds a bachelor's degree in European history from Wesleyan University; a master of arts in teaching in European and American history from University of California, Davis; and a doctorate in American history from University of California, Davis.

Erin Riley

Erin Riley is the Engineering and Design Lab director of the Greenwich Academy in Greenwich, Connecticut, United States, a girls school serving grades preK through high school. Riley, a visual artist and curriculum developer, currently teaches engineering and design in grades 4 through high school and works with colleagues of all grade levels on projects involving the design lab. Riley holds a bachelor of fine arts from University of Utah, a master of fine arts from Maryland Institute College of Art, and a certificate in art and design education from Pratt Institute.

Tracy Rudzitis

Tracy Rudzitis is the STEAM Lab facilitator at MS25 in New York City, United States. MS25 is a public middle school known as The Computer School, serving a diverse student population. Rudzitis's STEAM Lab class reaches three hundred sixth- and seventh-grade students each week. She also teaches a robotics class in an after-school program. She has taught middle school in the New York City public school system for fourteen years with a focus on digital media, computer programming, and robotics. In 2012, Rudzitis created a modest makerspace and invited students to drop by during their lunch hour to explore. This informal program has grown to be a fully equipped lab that often serves seventy students during their lunch period. Outside the classroom, she is a leader of the NYC Scratch Day, the NYC Robo-Expo, and the NYC STEAM Think Tank. She holds a master of fine arts from the Visual Studies Workshop in Rochester, New York.

Mark Schreiber

Mark Schreiber is the director of innovation and design and a teacher of design and engineering at the American School in Tokyo, a preK–12 independent school. His work involves integrating making into all subjects and training staff in design and fabrication. He oversees an elementary lab, a robotics lab, two middle school labs, and two high school labs. Prior to relocating to Japan, Schreiber was the director of technology and home school enrichment at Frontier Academy, a charter school in Greeley, Colorado, United States. He has fifteen years experience teaching design and engineering. He holds a bachelor of arts in technology education and industrial technology, and a master's in construction, technology, and engineering education from Colorado State University. He is a member of MIT's international Fab Lab network. In addition to his work in education, he is the owner of DesignCase Consulting in Fort Collins, Colorado.

Susanna Tesconi

Susanna Tesconi is a learning environments designer and researcher at LABoral Art and Industrial Creation Centre, Gijon [Asturias], Spain, and the Department of Applied Pedagogy, Autonomous University of Barcelona. LABoral is an art institution that focuses on the intersection of art, science, and technology. In partnership with the Ministry Education of Asturias, LABoral has developed programming for primary and secondary levels. As a doctoral candidate at the Autonomous University of Barcelona, she teaches digital fabrication for educational settings to primary school student teachers. She is also conducting research on the transformative potential of making in teacher education. Tesconi holds a degree in philosophy of language from Universita degli Studi di Pisa, Italy, a postgraduate degree in interaction design from the Universitat Pompeu Fabra in Barcelona, and a master's degree in educational research from the Autonomous University of Barcelona.

Nalin Tutiyaphuengprasert

Nalin Tutiyaphuengprasert is senior vice provost of Darunsikkhalai School for Innovative Learning, a constructionist grade 1–12 pilot school at King Mongkut's University of Technology Thonburi, in Bangkok, Thailand. Her program, the first FabLearn Labs initiative in Asia, began in 2013 as a collaborative project with the Transformative Learning Technology Lab at Stanford's Graduate School of Education. As the FabLearn Lab project manager, Tutiyaphuengprasert teaches students in grades 1–12 and provides professional development for faculty plus teachers from other institutions. She is also the coordinator between Thailand and Stanford University for many collaborative projects and research in Thailand. She holds a master's degree from the Stanford Graduate School of Education's Learning, Design, and Technology program; a master's degree in business administration from Chulalongkorn University; and a bachelor's in journalism from Thammasat University.

Aaron Vanderwerff

Aaron Vanderwerff is the Creativity Lab director at Lighthouse Community Charter School, a K–12 public charter school serving low-income students of color in Oakland, California, United States. His work involves helping educators at all grade levels integrate making into their curriculum. Vanderwerff has taught high school science in the Bay Area for over ten years. At Lighthouse, he has taught chemistry, physics, and robotics. He holds a bachelor's degree in electrical engineering from the University of Illinois and a master's in education from Mills College.

Juliet Wanyiri

Juliet Wanyiri is the founder of Foondi Workshops in Nairobi, Kenya, which runs collaborative design workshops. Wanyiri is an electrical engineer and is an organizer and alumna of the International Development Design Summit (IDDS), an annual design and innovation summit organized by MIT's design lab. Wanyiri is a member of the 2016 IDIN Workshop Fellowship program. Prior to this, Wanyiri was the director of Gearbox makerspace. She was also part of the engineering team behind BRCK.

Foreword

by Paulo Blikstein

You cannot think about thinking without thinking about what Seymour Papert would think. There is a paradox in education: the closer the world comes to realizing Seymour Papert's vision, the less is his work remembered. In a sense, this is perhaps the best outcome possible for a visionary—when what used to be radical becomes a mainstream idea. Papert and his collaborators dreamed up a world where all children would be able to program and "make"—except that they did it in 1968.

If a historian were to draw a line connecting Piaget's work on developmental psychology to today's trends in educational technology, the line would simply be labeled *Papert*. Seymour Papert has been at the center of three seismic events in research: child development, artificial intelligence, and technologies for education. He was born on February 29, 1928, in Pretoria, South Africa. He was a philosophy student at South Africa's University of Witwatersrand, where he received a PhD in mathematics in 1952. He proceeded to St. John's College at Cambridge, where he earned a second PhD in 1958. As part of his doctoral work, he had spent time at the Henri Poincaré Institute in Paris, where he would meet Jean Piaget. He would spend four years working under Piaget at the University of Geneva and was profoundly influenced by Piaget's work on how children make sense of the world—not as "miniature adults" but as active theory builders. Papert wrote in 1991 a wonderful definition of what the "maker movement" would reinvent in the 2000s:

> Constructionism shares constructivism's connotation of learning as "building knowledge structures." … It then adds the idea that this happens especially felicitously in a context where the learner is engaged in constructing a public entity.

During his time in Geneva, Papert had made another serendipitous connection: in 1960 he met Marvin Minsky. Later with Minsky, Papert cofounded the Massachusetts Institute of Technology (MIT) Artificial Intelligence Laboratory and the MIT Media Lab.

If one were to, a bit unfairly, measure Papert's career by the sheer number of people a project touched, Logo would eclipse all other achievements. In 1968, Papert, Cynthia Solomon, Daniel Bobrow, and Wally Feurzeig crafted Logo, a revolutionary programming language, the first designed for children. His vision, almost fifty years ago, was that children should be programming the computer rather than being programmed by it. Papert's work entered mainstream consciousness in 1980, with the publication of the seminal book *Mindstorms: Children, Computers, and Powerful Ideas*. His Epistemology and Learning Group at MIT attracted a legion of bright students and researchers who, over the next decades, would bring to millions of children computer programming (Scratch), robotics (LEGO, Cricket, Pico Cricket, Makey Makey), multiagent modeling (NetLogo), cybernetics, system dynamics, and digital fabrication. Because of Papert's book, of course, the LEGO company named its robotics kit "Mindstorms."

His awareness that children's cognitive evolution requires designing rich tool kits and environments rather than force-feeding knowledge has set the tone for decades of research. The combination of developmental psychology, artificial intelligence, and technology proved to be extremely powerful. Through a fortuitous historical accident, a disciple of Piaget bumped into Marvin Minsky, ended up at MIT, and gave us Logo and Mindstorms.

If you want to do work on computational literacy, programming for children, or the maker movement, there is no way to ignore Papert. His extended team laid out the theoretical and technological foundations for the popularity of these ideas today. Instead of allowing this story to be forgotten, we should instead establish a culture in which we don't reinvent the wheel every ten years but stand on the shoulders of our giant Logo turtles.

Constructionism has, at its heart, a desire not to revise but to invert the world of curriculum-driven instruction. One of the main lessons is that there can't be making without sense making. But although this might sound radical, the first step is to acknowledge that constructionism has won the battle for the minds. Everyday we see people, children, and parents getting excited about the things they can see, program, make, and do together. The Maker Faire is a worldwide exhibition of constructionism. There are literally hundreds of schools starting fab labs and maker-spaces. Scratch and NetLogo are used by millions of children and adults in fifty languages. Thousands of schools have robotics programs. Papert won. But now we have to claim his victory and tell the world, for academic and historic justice, that many of these ideas were first thought out by him. But we also have to announce what's next and our new visions. And what is next? We should not take Papert's ideas as a finished and unquestionable canon but as the start of a much larger project.

In the famous "Gears of My Childhood" preface to *Mindstorms*, Papert states what he has always considered "the fundamental fact about learning: anything is easy if you can assimilate it to your collection of models. If you can't, anything can be painfully difficult." Education needs a collection of models demonstrating the impact of implementing Papert's ideas in school. Maybe then they will not anymore be painfully hard to implement but a lot easier. This book is a collection of such models, written by visionary educators who took on the job of bringing constructionism to their schools, building labs, and creating activities, toolkits, and curricula. They understand that we are at a crossroads, where yet again two different philosophies of education battle: on one hand, the proponents of mass-produced instruction-ism, now powered by Internet video, and on the other, the advocates of the highly personal forms of learning that come from making, building, and creating one's own theories. At first sight, it seems like a lost fight between a few innovative teachers against multinational publishing companies and overhyped entrepreneurs. But this time I believe that there is a way to win. We might have to put aside our own idealized views of how things work and understand that overnight changes in education are hard—and that even Papert was a bit too optimistic about it. A more productive path might be, indeed, to create multiple models of implementation, assessment, and curriculum construction; document inspiring narratives of success or failure; and do rigorous research on the learning that happens. With enough of those models and proofs of existence, it will be increasingly less threatening for new teachers to join, new districts to embrace the ideas, and ultimately whole school systems to try to incorporate making and constructionism into their curriculum.

Maybe, after all, the revolution will not happen overnight but one school at a time. But until then it is our job to build those models, tell these stories, do the research, document the work, and tell the world about the incredible things students can do when they are empowered to build, think, and create.

Let's make Seymour Papert proud.

Constructionism in Action

The first section of this book is a collection of articles about how Seymour Papert's theory of learning, *constructionism*, combines with the modern tools and technologies of the maker movement to create new opportunities for learning. The FabLearn Fellows offer their views on various topics from the nature of learning to creating environments for children that foster deeper understandings and connections with powerful ideas. By placing these big ideas in real contexts of classrooms and other learning spaces, theory comes alive and vision becomes action.

From Name Tags to Lasting Artifacts: Fostering a Culture of Deep Projects

by Christa Flores

Introduction

Much hype has been made about incorporating *design* or *design thinking* into education, but what is design, and why is it "suddenly" a valued twenty-first century concept in education? Anyone who has taken a design thinking workshop knows that little is gained from a one-hour design cycle, especially those based on product development that may or may not be a sustainable use of resources. On the other hand, understanding the actual process of design through first-hand practice requires time, a lot of time—years in some cases. That being the case, are schools that push design into their programs allowing students to know more than the terms of design (such as *brainstorm*, *iterate*, and *empathy*), or are they truly teaching the value and intricacy of the design process (fig. 1.1)? This article was inspired by Paulo Blikstein's writings on design and making in education (Blikstein 2016).

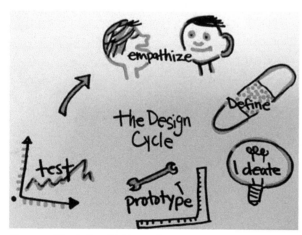

Figure 1.1: The design-thinking cycle.

The design process: Design thinking or design science

Anyone can search the Internet for "design thinking" to discover the term is rooted in the product design industry, which grew out of Stanford's d.school. David Kelly, one of the cofathers of design thinking, is a revolutionary thinker; his "human-centered" approach to design is more than colorful sticky notes and whiteboard doodles. Design thinking is based on an older idea referred to as *design science* or the *sciences of the artificial*.

"The central task of a natural science," according to Herbert Simon (1969), "is to make the world commonplace, to show that complexity, correctly viewed, is only a mask for simplicity; to find pattern hidden in chaos." The sciences of the natural sought to make the wonderful "not incomprehensible," argues Simon, who then describes the *artificial* as any artifact created by man. Design thinking evolved from a perspective that the act of design is the use of thinking routines applied to the natural sciences, to inform how to construct artificial means for humans to interface with the world. With the addition of the concept of empathy, deep listening, or storytelling, design thinking can and should be more than a mindless march to mass produce.

In *How Designers Think: The Design Process Demystified*, architect and design researcher Bryan Lawson argues that applying the design process is a skill of the mind, akin to riding a bike or playing an instrument. His research suggests that thinking like a designer can compliment thinking like a scientist when it comes to problem solving with constraints (Lawson 1997).

For Kenya Hara "There are an unlimited number of ways of thinking and perceiving. In my understanding, to design is to intentionally apply to ordinary objects, phenomena, and communication, the essence of these innumerable ways of thinking and perceiving." Design in this sense is a mind-set, a lens through which you can see the infinite layers of detail in the world (Hara 2011).

The design process allows the designer to apply the knowledge from the natural sciences to a creative science. The creation of the artificial, whether it be room temperature, a modernist chair, or a school system, is solution finding, armed with scientific knowledge—with or without a strong focus on the user. Placing the user at the center of why we make things brings to the engineering process a story. Stories create connections and allow students to empathize—and in turn gain diverse perspectives of the world they live in.

Making for change: The value of design in school

The East Bay School for Boys (EBSB) in Berkeley, California, has an impressive metal arts program. At this five-year-young, agile, middle school serving under one hundred students, projects allow boys to identify with their culture and their emotional and physical selves; they have *capoeira* and beekeeping classes, and they can make a half-pipe skate ramp and their own steel knives. In some projects boys work with local homeless residents; others gain empowerment through capstones based on a superhero theme for social justice.

Kyle Metzner and David Clifford are the creative minds behind the EBSB design-thinking program. Kyle comes from a professional background in design and fabrication, and David has a fellowship at the Stanford d.school, where he is part of a cohort of individuals "working in a variety of ways to invent, disrupt, and innovate in and around complex social systems." The value of teaching the design process, claims Kyle, is that "you cannot hand hold a student through the design process" (fig. 1.2). Design is the ultimate test of creativity and willingness to iterate.

In problem-based science classes at Hillbrook School in Los Gatos, California, in a four-month design project referred to as the "spring hard problem," students ages ten and eleven follow four simple rules or prompts. At the end of the school year, they grade themselves on the design

Figure 1.2: Kyle Metzner explains the blacksmithing curriculum and how it has informed the students in areas ranging from conscientious consumption and molecular structure to ancient cultures.

and engineering process by arguing for a Pass or Fail grade. This construction of an argument, as well as a detailed log of skills and topics employed to solve problems, is another avenue for practicing the design process. Writing is a craft to be honed, just like design skills or using tools. We use terms such as *craftsmanship* when working with words or wood.

Google Docs is a valuable tool when working on process, as this platform offers students easily accessible tools for self-publishing as well as a quick and permanent means for teachers to give feedback.

When my students invent, they take ownership over an idea, then face real-world problems on their route to making their idea come to life (figs. 1.3–1.5).

At the middle school level the design process is a creative exploration of hard, yet fun, problems (rigor + risk + reward), positive identity formation (*I am creative, I am a scientist, I can solve problems*), and collaborative learning that questions the status quo. Add responsible resource management and exposure to social justice issues, and design becomes a thinking tool for empowerment and stewardship. These are a few reasons why the design process is incorporated into the sciences at Hillbrook School.

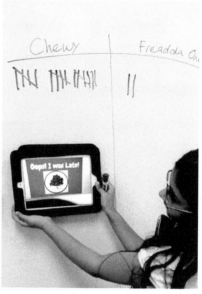

Figure 1.3: Measure twice, cut—well, it depends. The iterative process almost never follows a straight line.

Figure 1.4: Small successes add up to big solutions. This student is endeavoring to build a 60+ light display using a single wall-outlet plug with a 12-volt output from an e-waste pile.

Figure 1.5: Science through survey for peer feedback. This was the winning design for the redesign of the Hillbrook Late Pass. The community decides what quality and beauty are.

References

Blikstein, P., & Worsley, M. (2016). Children are not hackers: Building a culture of powerful ideas, deep learning, and equity in the maker movement. In E. Halverson, K. Peppler, & Y. Kafai (Eds.), *Makeology: Makerspaces as learning environments (Volume 1)*. London, UK: Routledge.

Hara, K. (2011). *Designing design*. Zurich, Switzerland: Lars Muller Publishers.

Lawson, B. (1997). *How designers think: The design process demystified*. Oxford, UK: Architectural.

Simon, H. A. (1969). *The sciences of the artificial*. Cambridge, MA: MIT Press.

Thoughts on Learning and Engagement and the Pluto New Horizons Mission

by Tracy Rudzitis

I sat next to one of my sixth-grade students, J., as he flipped though one of his favorite books, a large picture book of the planets and their moons. This book accompanied him to our makerspace in the computer lab every day so he could refer to it. He showed me some of his favorite parts and read passages to me as he held a model of one of the moons described in the book (fig. 2.1).

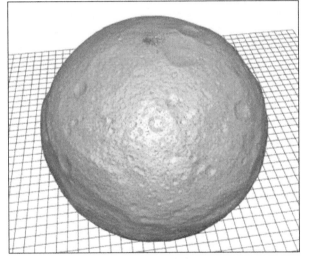

Figure 2.1: Student-designed 3D model of a moon.

J. designed this moon in Tinkercad and had printed it out using the 3D printer in the lab. It was just one of a half-dozen moons or planets that he had designed and printed. Ranging in size from a ping-pong ball to a tennis ball, they didn't really look like much, but when J. described the features and the characteristics of the moon and how he was able to translate that into his own design and then print it and hold it, the shape took on incredible meaning.

Watching J. and listening to him read about some of his favorite moons, I witnessed an intensity for learning and a motivation for uncovering more information and exploring creative ways to be further engaged. I saw him grasping a physical object of his own creation, even if it was not something he was actively referring to as he was reading.

NASA provides some outstanding free 3D resources for those interested in space and space exploration.[1] The New Horizons Pluto flyby gave us all an opportunity to rekindle our fascination with outer space.

Students can explore their interests in three dimensions, and students like J. can imagine these faraway worlds in a more personalized and immediate way through designing their own 3D models based on their own imaginations, research, and picture books. Teachers can also explore and share with their students the many resources about how 3D printing technology and materials are used in the space program.[2]

Notes

1. nasa3d.arc.nasa.gov
2. nasa.gov/topics/technology manufacturing -materials-3d/index.html

What Do People Learn from Using Digital Fabrication Tools?

by Erin Riley

While conceiving an idea and shepherding it into a tangible form is significant, it is important to be able to articulate its value within an educational setting (fig. 3.1). It's also important to reveal the many stages in digital fabrication, especially illuminating the often hidden design process where much of the learning takes place.

Digital fabrication, which begins with digital design and ends with output from a fabrication machine, parallels predigital processes for making things. A laser cutter or a Computer Numerical Control (CNC) router cuts designs in a manner similar to a scroll saw. A sculptor can build up clay in an additive approach just as a 3D printer lays down lines of plastic or chisels marble with a subtractive approach as the CNC milling machine would carve wax. Digital design adds precision, scaling, cross-machine capabilities, and reproducibility to the mix (fig. 3.2).

Figure 3.1: Students ready for action in the fabrication lab.

Those working with students using these tools know that digital fabrication is the merging of the human with the technical. The result is a creative product formed from their ideas and executed through a series of complex design decisions.

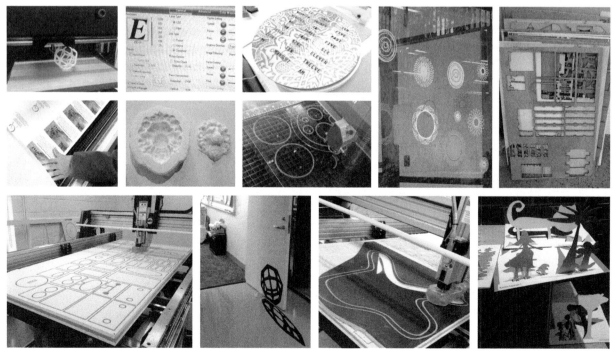

Figure 3.2: A variety of student work.

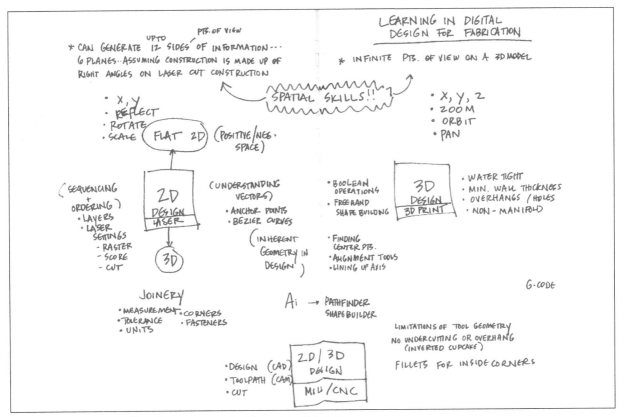

Figure 3.3: A concept map of learning outcomes gained from digital fabrication.

Through 2D and 3D design and making, students develop multiple skills, not only in growing proficiency with 2D and 3D design, but also in spatial development and a variety of mathematical concepts (fig 3.3).

Students' learning goes beyond acquiring skills and includes strengthening critical thinking as an outgrowth of working through design and fabrication problems. Gaining facility, and refining one's ability to be mindful, active learning isn't limited to digital fabrication; making in general promotes curiosity-driven, self-directed, creative learning.

Skills-based learning: 2D and 3D design and spatial development

So what does one actually learn from digital fabrication? And what is the breakdown of skills acquired through the process of digital design and production, including controlling the machine to make that product? An online forum for teachers using digital fabrication tools, the K–12 Fab Labs and Makerspaces Google group,[1] addressed a similar topic. Themes that included the development of spatial reasoning, math concepts, and 2D/3D design emerged. Many of these teachers saw many layers of learning embedded in the design-to-making process.

A simple way of looking at the skills-based learning that occurs in digital fabrication is to look at each machine and the learning and process skills learned in designing for that machine.

3D printer
Learning from the design process
- Math and spatial reasoning: navigating the 3D design environment, designing on all sides (X, Y, and Z), alignment tools, geometric shape building, dividing and combining, measurement tools, units, scale, ratio, rotating, mirroring, Boolean operations, and precision

Learning from the fabrication process
- Machine operation: machine settings—raft, supports, infill
- Designing for the machine including its limitations: slicing a model into smaller parts that get attached later, designing supports like cones that can be cut off later, reorienting the model for better support
- Science behind the process: the technology of additive processes, slicing, G-code

Beginners can jump right into 3D printing with the help of user-friendly software like Tinkercad. The solid geometric forms students build with are watertight, which can alleviate certain printing problems and prevent frustrations later on. Complex forms are built up through manipulating positive and negative space and grouping. The learning curve for machine operation is low, and students can easily get involved in the entire design-through-fabrication process. Once students are comfortable navigating the 3D design space, they can translate their ideas into the 3D world. After a successful introduction to 3D printing, students are excited to attempt more complex projects.

Laser cutter

Learning from the design process:

2D

- Math and spatial reasoning: navigating 2D design environment (X and Y), geometric shape building, dividing and combining, measurement tools, units, scale, ratio, rotating, mirroring, positive and negative space, and precision
- Graphics: vector design, alignment tools
- Ordering, sequencing, and visualizing: layering for the sequence of etching and cutting

2D to 3D

- Math and spatial reasoning: joinery, visualizing the translation of 2D to 3D (from shape to form)

Learning from the machine cutting process:

- Machine operation: machine settings—stroke, fill, hairline, RGB black
- Science behind the process: laser technology

The laser cutter makes 2D and 3D objects. A laser cutter cuts (or etches) material in two dimensions, and flat objects can be made three dimensional by joining the pieces after they are cut. Designing for the laser cutter involves planning and generating these multiple pieces.

Students quickly begin 2D design by converting hand-drawn designs into vectors and outputting them to the laser. The next step is to learn to draw with basic 2D design program tools such as the shape-drawing tools, pen tool, and shape-builder tool in Adobe Illustrator.

When moving from 2D to 3D on the laser cutter, joinery comes into play. Here students refer to a timeless predigital skill that requires them to consider width of material; visualizing how flat pieces unfold and potentially fit together engages spatial skills.

CNC milling

Learning from the design process

2D

- Math and spatial reasoning: navigating 2D design environment (X and Y), alignment tools, geometric shape building, dividing and combining, measurement tools, units, scale, ratio, rotating, mirroring, positive and negative space, and precision
- Graphics: vector design
- Ordering, sequencing, and visualizing: layering for sequence of drilling, milling, and cutting

2D to 3D

- Math and spatial reasoning: joinery, visualizing the translation of 2D to 3D (from shape to form)

3D

- Math and spatial reasoning: navigating 3D design environment, designing on all sides (X, Y, and Z), alignment tools, geometric shape building, dividing and combining, measurement tools, units, scale, ratio, rotating, mirroring, Boolean operations

Learning from the fabrication machine process

- CNC routing and engraving software: tool paths: drill, profile, pocket, V-carve, 3D modeling, slicing, tool geometry, feeds and speeds, G-code, measuring
- Machine operation: loading stock; zeroing X, Y, and Z; switching tools
- Science behind the process: CNC and milling technology

A CNC machine cuts materials by moving a rotary cutter to remove material and create an object. The laser cutter and the CNC share many of the same design considerations; both require use of layers and sequencing when planning cuts, carving, drilling, and milling. There are limitations inherent in the geometry of the cutting tool that do not account for undercuts and corners. It

Figure 3.4: A variety of student work.

is also more complex on the machine side with the additional step of selecting appropriate cutting tools and using separate software to generate tool paths (fig 3.4).

An added level of learning on the CNC machine is the finish work involved with a woodworking project. Parts are tabbed into the material and require removal and filing. Some projects generate parts that later need connecting, clamping, filing, and sanding.

The skills acquired from design and fabrication have real-world applications in engineering, art, design, science, computer science, and math. In addition to these important skills, the culture of a makerspace itself can help students become independent learners driven by curiosity and intrinsic motivation. I experienced this myself as part of an early-user team involved with Greenwich Academy's establishment of a lab. Mastery of each machine and the unique design considerations required to output to them was new to me. This is what I learned:

I can teach myself to do this.

- I can learn how to design in 2D and 3D and use a machine to make that object by seeking out resources to help.
- Like with so many new and emerging technologies, there are many resources available. Books, websites, how-tos, and video tutorials are readily available for self-learning.

WHY THIS IS IMPORTANT FOR STUDENTS

- Self-directed learning is a practice that will serve students in all areas of their learning.

I can seek help to troubleshoot problems.

- If I can't find an answer to my question with the resources I have available, I can reach out to others.
- When I am really stuck, I can call someone, consult an online community, or bug friends at the local makerspace.

WHY THIS IS IMPORTANT FOR STUDENTS

- It teaches them that there is no shame in asking for help.

I can teach others to do this.

- Even if I'm not an expert, the knowledge I have can help others.
- When we opened our digital fabrication lab, we were all newbies in using the technology. Each one of us learned as we went along and had something to share with the group.

WHY THIS IS IMPORTANT FOR STUDENTS

- Students contribute to the collective knowledge base.

I can solve new problems.

- I can merge ideas, extrapolate, and find connections when I do not have a solution to my specific problem.
- Learning comes with all sorts of challenges. Maybe the software isn't compatible; maybe I have a Mac but they have a PC; perhaps what I am trying to do doesn't quite correlate with the resources I have at hand. We have all experienced a situation when we cannot neatly follow a step-by-step recipe to arrive at a solution. It forces us to dig a little deeper, perhaps learn something different but related, and by doing so, make the connection.

WHY THIS IS IMPORTANT FOR STUDENTS

- It encourages flexible, creative thinking. It provides opportunities for learning to be applied to a situation in a new or indirect way.

Learning is not a one-time thing.

- I can tackle increasingly complex problems.
- The iterative nature of these kinds of projects plus the unlimited versatility of these tools creates a positive reinforcement cycle.

WHY THIS IS IMPORTANT FOR STUDENTS

- Even when tools are difficult to use, or don't work as expected, students learn to adjust and accommodate their designs to these constraints. As they use the tools more, they increase their competency and therefore can tackle more complex designs.

It's okay to go on a tangent with learning.

- I find more opportunities to learn when teaching myself.
- The journey of self-learning opens the door to new ideas. Stumbling upon projects, processes, and new tools is the starting point for idea generation. If I don't know exactly how to get to my goal, there is room to move off course.

WHY THIS IS IMPORTANT FOR STUDENTS

- Students follow their interests in the process of learning. Students learn there is more than "one right answer."

In the quest to answer a question, I find myself with more questions.

- The more I learn, the more questions I have.
- Perhaps it has something to do with wanting to find connections between ideas, but I find as I seek answers to questions, more emerge.

WHY THIS IS IMPORTANT FOR STUDENTS

- Learning fuels curiosity.

I can learn my way.

- There are different ways to achieve the same goal.
- Learning is personal when you can craft your own strategies for solving a problem. They may not always be the most efficient, but they are yours and become part of your larger body of knowledge. As new ways of doing something are adopted, an old strategy can be applied or modified to future situations and becomes part of a creative problem-solving vocabulary.

WHY THIS IS IMPORTANT FOR STUDENTS

- Creative, personally meaningful solutions are prized.

Making, or digital fabrication in schools, is a creative process. Students learn all sorts of skills and ways of thinking that help them become better learners. Whether Boolean operations or how to research problems, the main thing students learn is how to navigate the process of going from idea stage to final object (fig. 3.5).

Note

1. K12makers.com

Figure 3.5: Grades 4 and 11 working together on digital fabrication problems.

Launching Boats

by Erin Riley

I once heard teaching compared to the act of launching boats. What a nice visual is evoked by that metaphor. We can think of the work we do in our makerspaces as a similar process to preparing for, and ultimately taking off, on a self-guided journey: students captain the ship, and teachers watch from the shore.

Learning through play

Children learn through play and exploration. From floating sticks downstream to ducks in the tub, early lessons in how the world works come from play (fig. 4.1). Could this be the first step in the progression toward mastery? By building upon play, a mode of learning that is rooted in curiosity and joy, we can engage our students in a truly authentic way. For instance, a project involving electronics can be launched with a session on

circuit boards,[1] or woodworking with a one-block challenge.[2] Both of these activities originate from two excellent resources for exploration-based maker activities: the Tinkering Studio at the Exploratorium,[3] and the Makerspace at the New York Hall of Science.[4]

Mastery: Learning the ropes

Play sparks interest. Interest drives the desire for mastery. Practicing and gaining mastery build confidence. The teacher strives to find the balance between guidance and autonomy. Excitement over making connections, getting better at making things, completing projects, and overcoming obstacles is the process that builds confidence as students move toward full independence.

At Greenwich Academy in Greenwich, Connecticut, one student documented in her maker portfolio her process for building a paper circuit project including challenges and breakthroughs along the way. She wrote:

> A great maker is not only one who is willing to make mistakes but one who is willing to still think big in spite of the threat of mistakes. In keeping with that theme, I decided to create an easy button.
>
> I even left a little room for myself to think big during the project. While pasting copper wires down, I realized I was missing an essential element to my Think Big button, a noise component. I remember my favorite part of the Staples Easy button was the little phrase it spit out each time you pressed it.
>
> So I went to CVS, bought a singing card, and removed the sound circuit. The circuit contained a circuit board with an attached speaker. Probably the hardest part of the whole project was trying to figure out how to get the sound to stop.

Figure 4.1: Learning should be fun.

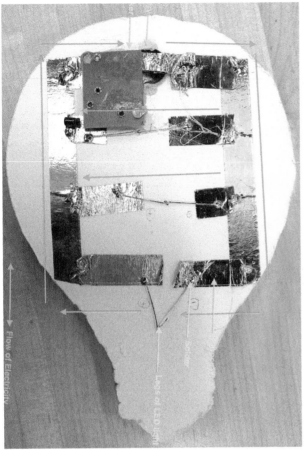

Figure 4.2: Think Big button design.

After much trial and error, I found the happy medium that required me to extend the length of the copper switch so it nestled in the center of the battery and placed the clip for the sound right next to the copper.

This process has not only yielded a successful project but a successful [me]. It shows that I am one step closer to achieving my goal as a confident maker (fig 4.2).

On her journey toward understanding her circuit, this student recognized an increase in her confidence. She was well on her way toward steering the ship. The teacher stepped back and the student took the lead.

The launch and the teacher at the shore

Another student's paper circuit project evolved into artistic handmade paper circuit cards. Accomplished in the art studio, she found her voice through the fusion of media to express her ideas. In this case, the student built upon a strong knowledge of art-and-craft process, and incorporated an emerging skill base in electronics (fig. 4.3).

The next object she made, a word clock (fig. 4.4) built around Doug's Word Clocks board,[5] included handmade marbled paper in the enclosure, and her documentation revealed the

Figure 4.3: Hand-embossed card with an LED circuit.

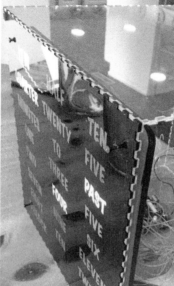

Figure 4.4: Transparent word clock enclosure design with marbled paper.

carefully considered aesthetic and design decisions she made while demonstrating confidence and independence with electronics.

Her reflection about learning in the lab underscored the importance of building skills on her way to becoming an independent maker. She wrote:

> By the end of this course, I would like to be a maker that thinks beyond "outside of the box." To me this means challenging the norms, breaking patterns, and figuring out new ways. The maker I want to be is one that never stops thinking. Even outside of the lab, I want to be thinking about how to take my projects one step further than my mental capacity. Furthermore, I also believe it is important to first build a strong platform on which to build from. I also think it is important to keep an open mind as anything is truly possible. Inside the lab with limitless resources, I believe with enough drive, passion, and learning I will become just that.

Notes

1. tinkering.exploratorium.edu/circuit-boards
2. makerspace.nysci.org/oneblockchallenge
3. tinkering.exploratorium.edu
4. makerspace.nysci.org
5. dougswordclocks.com

Fostering a Constructionist Learning Environment: The Qualities of a Maker Educator

by **Christa Flores**

Constructionism is not interested in pitting serious against playful but instead finds ways to live at the intersection of the two.   —Paulo Blikstein

In Paulo Blikstein and Marcelo Worsley's chapter in *Makeology* (2016), the power of the culture of making is said to be highly dependent on the pedagogical style and attitude of the teacher. Fostering a constructionist learning environment is no small charge. Once established, however, this environment offers a world of learning experiences that challenge the status quo of teaching and learning seen in most schools (fig. 5.1; Papert and Harel 1991).

What qualities would a teacher possess in a constructionist environment, and how would these superheroes behave? The following descriptions are the top-five qualities and behaviors to keep in your tool kit for fostering a constructionist learning environment.[1]

Figure 5.1: A constructionist classroom is highly dependent on culture.

Keep it brief, relevant, and open

Gary Stager and Sylvia Martinez have a great approach to lesson planning for maker education—the use of prompts instead of teacher-led and cookie-cutter curricula for best results in constructionism. Good prompts are simple enough for kids to understand, vague enough to allow a diverse and open array of solutions, and immune to standardized testing (Martinez and Stager 2013). Prompts mirror the effect of using essential questions to deepen engagement, understanding, and love of learning. Like essential questions, prompts also allow for the natural integration of math, science, technology, the fine and performing arts, social studies, and language arts. In other words, relevant and real problems look like real life.

Model the maker mindset

Be willing to colearn; see the use of technology as an opportunity rather than an insurmountable challenge. Gary Stager is famous for saying, "You can't teach twenty-first century learners if you haven't learned this century." Erin Riley notes that makerspaces are not your everyday classroom environment: "The makerspace attracts those kinds of teachers willing to take a risk in teaching old content in a new way." Teachers have to be ready to throw out what simply looks like "good teaching" for more effective teaching, which will look different in different settings. It might look like a play, a concert, a cave-mapping robot, or a scratch video game. The list is endless.

Act like a scientist

You are exploring new territory as a maker educator. Record using images, self-reflections, portfolios, and any tool at your disposal to reveal how and what your students are learning. Mark Schreiber reminds us that one of our roles is "to assess how this works, which is better or complementary to the current practices of our peers in their classrooms." Do not be intimidated by testing something that has never been done. A scientist revels in the unknown. Constructionism and making may offer a better vision of school and learning. Let's prove it together by showing and sharing work (Educator Innovator 2015).

Reward curiosity and passion with rigor

Fredrick Douglas is famed for stating "Without struggle there is no progress." Take out *progress* and insert *learning*, and you have a recipe for what constructionism feels like. Never tell students their ideas are too hard or above grade level. Let them discover their own natural boundaries and when they get stuck, brainstorm possible solutions with them or in a team. This concept of allowing learners to step beyond themselves is explained in Vygotsky's zone of proximal development as an essential element of learning (Vygotsky 1978).

Keep it safe

Social emotional learning is a large part of what we do as educators. Fostering a safe space that values new ideas, nontraditional uses for tools and materials, and taking risks to solve hard problems is working against the inevitable consequences of more traditional systems of teaching and learning. What does keeping it safe look like in real terms? According to Falbel, "Creating a safe space for students to learn includes a welcoming, friendly space that is as free as possible from the pressures of time" (1993). Kids need time to be creative; show your value for this skill by devoting time to foster it. Lastly, a safe environment is one in which students participate in their own assessment, allowing them to see its value and to gain literacy and autonomy through it. Judgment slips away in the face of critical feedback, allowing the sharing of ideas to be a rewarding part of their learning journey.

Note

1. Thank you to FabLearn Fellows Mark Schreiber and Erin Riley for their feedback. They are quoted in this chapter from a FabLearn Fellows small group meeting held on April 7, 2015.

References

Blikstein, P., & Worsley, M. (2016). Children are not hackers: Building a culture of powerful ideas, deep learning, and equity in the maker movement. In E. Halverson, K. Peppler, & Y. Kafai (Eds.), *Makeology: Makerspaces as learning environments (Volume 1)*. London, UK: Routledge.

Educator Innovator (Producer). (2015, May 4). *Learning by making: An introduction to constructionism.* [Video]. Available from youtube.com/watch?v=DCSMvGB-sVA

Falbel, A. (1993). *Constructionism: Tools to build (and think) with.* Toronto, Canada: LEGO DACTA.

Martinez, S. L., & Stager, G. (2013). What makes a good project? In *Invent to learn: Making, tinkering, and engineering the classroom.* Torrance, CA: Constructing Modern Knowledge Press.

Papert, S., & Harel, I. (1991). Situating constructionism. In S. Papert & I. Harel (Eds.), *Constructionism*. Westport, CT: Ablex Publishing Corporation.

Vygotsky, L. S. (1978). *Mind in society: The development of higher psychological processes* (14th ed.). Cambridge, MA: Harvard University Press.

STEM, STEAM, and Making

by Tracy Rudzitis

What do these words mean? We know that *STEM* stands for "science, technology, engineering, and math," and *STEAM* represents adding "arts" to these subjects. *Making* is a shortcut for talking about hands-on, minds-on learning, especially with new technology. But how are they interpreted by teachers, administrators, students, and politicians?

In a number of discussions surrounding this question, although the conversations are genuine and in most cases have the best interests of students and learning in mind, there can be a wide range of perspectives and responses to these questions. Many times the conversations start to focus on questions such as "How can we create a STEAM curriculum that will prepare students for the AP physics exam?"

Perhaps it is time to break away from the idea that studying for and passing the AP physics exam defines a rich and engaging inquiry-based experience. Instead of asking if a STEAM or maker program will allow students to score well on an exam, we should be asking how the STEAM or maker program will foster a genuine love for investigation, for asking questions, and for curiosity and engagement about the world we live in. How can infusing a hands-on, open-ended experience allow students to discover and attempt to manipulate their world, while learning and experiencing the overarching concepts that make up a science (or math, etc.) curriculum (fig. 6.1)?

We have the momentum to alter the way that learning takes place in schools. So many have jumped on the maker bandwagon, and the STEM/STEAM acronyms are everywhere in the news. These new opportunities and ways to experience learning should remain true to the spirit in which they exist and not be diluted or changed because

Figure 6.1: Hands-on science.

existing curricula and pedagogy are being imposed upon them. It is important to have resources at hand for those interested in understanding more about the maker movement and how it is situated in pedagogy and learning theories.

Hands-on and inquiry-based exploration is nothing new to education, but one could get the impression that it is a brand new idea in the data-driven, test-prep environment that most schools are deeply entrenched in. In *Invent to Learn Making, Tinkering, and Engineering in the Classroom* (2013) the first chapter is dedicated to the history of making. It illustrates how making meaning through the exploration of materials is not a new concept but one with a rich and varied past. It is important that as educators we are aware of this history, and it should inform our approaches to teaching and making in our classrooms and be a part of this current dialogue on making.

One hundred years ago John Dewey (1916, 1938) wrote of the importance of creating meaningful experiences for students from which knowledge emerges. His idea that learning is social and the classroom should be a social environment where ideas and knowledge are constructed and shared as a community could be the mantra of any modern-day makerspace and for any age group.

Seymour Papert's constructionism is also rooted in the social experience: "Important concepts are consciously engaged and public entity. Constructionism is not just learning-by-doing, but engaging reflexively and socially in the task. Both the creation process and the produced artifacts ought to be socially shared" (Dougiamas 1998).

But even with such a rich history of maker pedagogy, many educators are unaware of—or don't trust—the methodology or process of children learning without being directly and explicitly told what it is they are supposed to be learning. In an excellent essay on constructivism and constructionism, Papert and Harel (1991) go into great detail about the nature of knowledge versus the nature of knowing. This article is just one of many possible starting points for these discussions on STEM, STEAM, and making that are happening in so many schools and districts.

How can we bring to the forefront the educators who do have successful programs where students are actively engaged in this way of learning—whose students are immersed in authentic and genuine projects that are meaningful to them? Educators who believe in the power of the maker movement can be instrumental in bringing change to the dominant pedagogical practice of teacher-disseminated knowledge and data-driven standards and testing that is so prevalent in this country right now, by creating spaces for this important dialogue.

Instead of situating STEAM and making into a traditional pedagogical framework of teaching and assessment, it must remain true to the spirit of making. Within the educational environment it is important that hands-on inquiry and discovery learning reference the work and research of constructivists and constructionists that have gone before.

References

Dewey, J. (1916). *Democracy and education*. New York, NY: Macmillan. Retrieved from archive.org/details /DemocracyAndEducation_201507

Dewey, J. (1938). *Experience and education*. New York, NY: Touchstone.

Dougiamas, M. (1998). "A journey into constructivism." Retrieved from dougiamas.com /archives/a-journey-into-constructivism/

Martinez, S. L., & Stager, G. (2013). *Invent to learn: Making, tinkering, and engineering the classroom*. Torrance, CA: Constructing Modern Knowledge Press.

Papert, S., & Harel, I. (1991). Situating constructionism. In S. Papert & I. Harel (Eds.), *Constructionism*. Westport, CT: Ablex Publishing Corporation.

The Power of Making What You Can Imagine

by Erin Riley

While teaching an upper-level drawing class, I noticed that some students were struggling to understand 3D space on the 2D drawing plane. In an effort to help these and future students, I reimagined a way of keeping track of studio projects based on where they might be organized by their 2D- to 3D-ness on a spectrum, and identifying the sorts of visualization that would be involved as they cross into other spatial forms. My notes—part curriculum development, part brainstorm, part webbing structure—took the form of mind maps, which helped to organize my ideas (fig. 7.1). This became a way of thinking about art, design, and making activities that I use in the Engineering and Design Lab and art studio today.

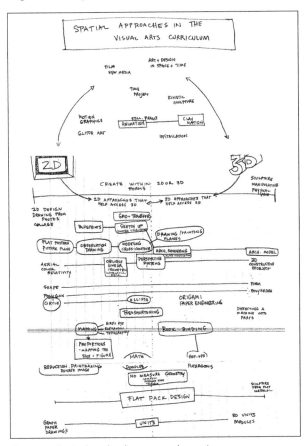

Figure 7.1: Curriculum development and mapping.

The mind's eye

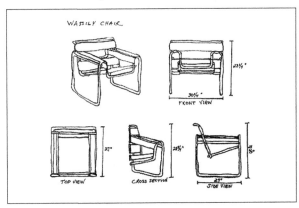

Figure 7.2: Student orthographic projection.

Moving back and forth between 2D and 3D approaches encourages mental visualization and strengthens spatial skills (fig. 7.2). Providing opportunities to practice translating mental imagery into the physical world empowers makers. An architecture student might undergo this process, accessing the idea in two dimensions by drawing a quick sketch of a structure and developing the visual idea to include floor plans, elevations, cross sections, and linear perspective renderings. Eventually the idea is brought into the physical world through the creation of a 3D model. The student utilizes mental visualization moving from 2D to 3D representation, first by drawing, then with physical construction to execute a design idea. A reverse approach is used in a project designed for middle school students: Think Like an Architect, Draw Like an Engineer (see article 22).

One lab project used a 3D entry point as students prototyped iPhone amplifier designs out of foam, cardboard, and recyclable materials (fig. 7.3). The prototypes were tested for amplification. Before moving onto a sketch, students had to translate their design idea into a second prototype using flat material stacked and configured. The material had to be easy to cut and build with. Stale toast was our choice for this design challenge. Moving from 3D to 2D, students drew plans of their designs, considering how each layer would register to create a three-dimensional object. They redrew their flat designs in Adobe Illustrator, and then these design files were compiled and cut on the CNC router. The final stage in this project brought the design back to the 3D world as students constructed their amplifiers. The sequence was as follows: 3D prototype → 3D stacking prototype → 3D drawing plan → 2D design plan as a drawing → 2D vector drawing → 3D construction.

Linking the eye, hand, and mind

It's standard teaching practice in the art field to describe the act of drawing as an exercise in linking the eye to the hand. Adding the mind to the mix gives makers access to mental imagery as well. Drawing is a visual language that unlocks students' power to bring their ideas into the physical world. The beauty is that the ideas do not have to be practical, functional, or realistic. Like Leonardo da Vinci and his inventions, many of which were precursors to modern designs, students can stretch their imaginations outside of the boundaries of the physical world and imagine what could be possible tomorrow.

To what end is all of this hard mental work of visualization and representing? STEM folks might say it's essential to engineering. Art folks might say it's essential to self-expression. Whether you are couching this question in the context of engineering design or hatching an idea untethered to function, we may simply want to frame it as essential to making.

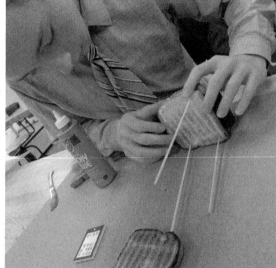

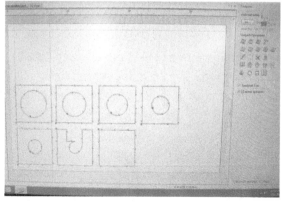

Figure 7.3: Prototyping iPhone amplifier designs.

The "Unstructured Classroom" and Other Misconceptions about Constructivist Learning

by Christa Flores

Is *student-centered* code for Lord of the Flies?

Ask any average kid what his or her favorite part of the school day is and you will probably get the answer *lunch* or *recess*. Kids love unstructured time because they have the privacy to fail while taking risks or learning how to be a social primate. At recess, kids have nearly 100 percent choice over what to do with their bodies, with the safe assumption that in case an injury does occur, an adult on duty will be on the scene in due time. Provide kids with a rich, not necessarily antiseptic, space to explore, such as a Scrapstore PlayPod,[1] and they teach us a lot about ingenuity, inclusivity and learning through play. Whether passionate about the physics of soccer or the game theory involved in the antics the day of a middle school dance, learning is experiential and self-directed at recess. Regardless of what passion takes over their choice time, we as adults trust them to make safe choices for the most part, and we respect their individuality (fig. 8.1). So why does that trust shift when those same children come into our classrooms?

Making is messy. From the outside, making looks unstructured, and this disrupts old ideas about what it means to support kids in school and to have good classroom management (fig. 8.2). In a 100 percent teacher-structured classroom, if a child struggles to learn a curriculum that was picked for his entire class and not for him personally, the child may be evaluated for having learning differences. If diagnosed with a learning difference, then he will be given an individualized learning plan. While this may sound awesome, in teacher code it means a set of instructions for the adults to practice with the child to ensure the success of the child in your class. An example of an

Figure 8.1: A workspace is a student's personal place.

instruction for the adult might be to write down every instruction for the child. Teachers are asked to be explicit regarding the modes for success in their classes to support the child. Sadly, this kind of system is designed to avoid failure more than leverage the individual interests or strengths of a child. While at first glance, this kind of teacher-led structure from which we normally spare high-achieving kids seems like good teaching. We even have the perfect term for it: *scaffolding*.

Solutions to support struggling students often attempt to solve a problem that was artificially created by teachers in the first place, leaving students' self-esteem in the wake. Here is where the value of making in the classroom becomes most clearly visible. Having the gift of watching students successfully learning and growing in areas that challenge them in a student-centered classroom, scaffolding and interventions may be nothing more than a lack of trust for a human's innate desire to learn

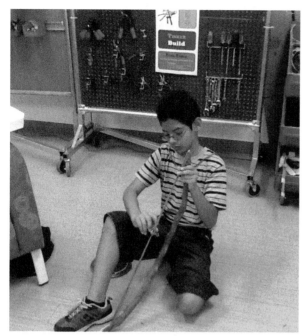

Figure 8.2: Like an orchestra, everyone does not play the same instrument.

what matters. Thankfully, I am not alone in my trust of children's innate desire to learn. We need look only at happy children on a playground or at the seminal research of Dr. Sugata Mitra on minimally invasive education[2] or listen to TED speaker and founder of San Francisco Brightworks Gever Tulley, coauthor of *50 Dangerous Things (You Should Let Your Children Do)*, to see that the right amount of danger through autonomy and real-world manipulatives such as playing with fire can foster key social emotional skills.

Giving kids agency and designing for self-direction does not come without its criticism, however, and anyone doing this work should take this into account. In the years that I have been teaching science through the lens of making, inventing, and problem solving, I have often heard my classroom, also known as the school's makerspace, referred to as "unstructured" by well-meaning adults. This harkens back to the discord between what we know progressive education can be versus what we envision when we think of a "progressive classroom." While working at a school in New York City that self-reported as a progressive school, the term *unstructured* was used a lot about lessons that were not 100 percent teacher directed. I also found it interesting to learn that families of color shopping for independent schools rarely hedge bets on their child's

education by considering schools that label themselves as progressive.

Self-directed learning environments are powerful tools to engage girls and minorities into science, but they also stand to foster feelings of alienation or frustration, too, if not facilitated well. In a blog post entitled "What a Girl Wants: Self-Directed Learning, Technology, and Gender" Sylvia Martinez links the importance of the self-directed nature of making in the classroom while pointing out the challenges it presents to fostering confidence in outsiders, such as girls in science or engineering classes. Sylvia points out that girls on average interact with self-direction differently than boys. Girls tend toward pleasing the teacher (or their friends or teammates) and avoid conflict over scarce resources, including the teacher's attention. "Teachers need to remember that their suggestions carry a great amount of weight. To counter this and encourage self-directed learning, teachers need to train themselves to offer neutral yet encouraging support for students to think outside the box," says Martinez (2014).

Due to the potentially negative image that the term *unstructured* elicits when talking about self-directed learning spaces, teachers of any discipline using a maker classroom should be ready to document student learning just like an ethnologist. They should get creative with documentation and take time to reflect on what they have seen.

There are skills to be gained in any maker-style curriculum on a spectrum from totally student driven to totally teacher directed. In my classroom I lean more toward student directed with a game-like structure. For any given unit—whether patterns, structures, or systems—I give a simple prompt that allows for the most diverse range of solutions for students to discover on their own. In game-like fashion, there are rules about deadlines, how to compose teams, and rules about when and how long play takes place (which is built into the school-day schedule).

There are levels of achievement and complexity of learning embedded into the system. These badges or levels are designed to remind us all to be mindful of safety, and they allow for a mentoring system where knowledge is democratic and passion based. Allowing students to chose the complexity with which they want to solve a problem is a side of autonomy about which we cross our fingers, but in the end, even when kids pick hard problems, they are experiencing something of value in that path full of potentially frustrating dead-ends.

Having the right amount of chaos and danger is essential for middle schoolers. It addresses socioemotional needs while sparking fierce passions for projects. Lastly, the authenticity of the work that kids do in an environment of constructing allows kids to see themselves as real inventors and engineers. In *Making Learning Whole: How Seven Principles of Teaching Can Transform Education*, David Perkins (2010) compares the kind of work kids can do in a fabrication lab environment to Little League baseball. Authenticity bridges mindsets in the fashion that a Little League baseball player can imagine being a professional baseball player. It feels real and it's age appropriate.

Finally, real science and engineering looks messy when done well. Trusting kids in the classroom is a good idea. Living with a little discomfort is part of the job description as it turns out. We model how to live with questions and the unknown for the sake of empathy and democracy in the classroom. For anyone practicing constructionism, you will soon see that there is no such thing as a lack of structure in a learning space. It only takes the eye of a designer and the inquiry of a scientist to see the complexity hidden within. When you find it, you will see that the complexity is deep and beautiful because it exists only when children are trusted to decide.

Notes

1. Time-lapse of a lunchtime playground rich with materials: youtube.com/watch?v=nqi1KyJJeKg
2. hole-in-the-wall.com/MIE.html

References

Martinez, S. (2014, November 3). What a girl wants: Self-directed learning, technology, and gender. [Blog post]. Retrieved from sylviamartinez.com/what-a-girl-wants-self-directed-learning-technology-and-gender/

Perkins, D. (2010). *Making learning whole: How seven principles of teaching can transform education*. San Francisco, CA: Jossey-Bass.

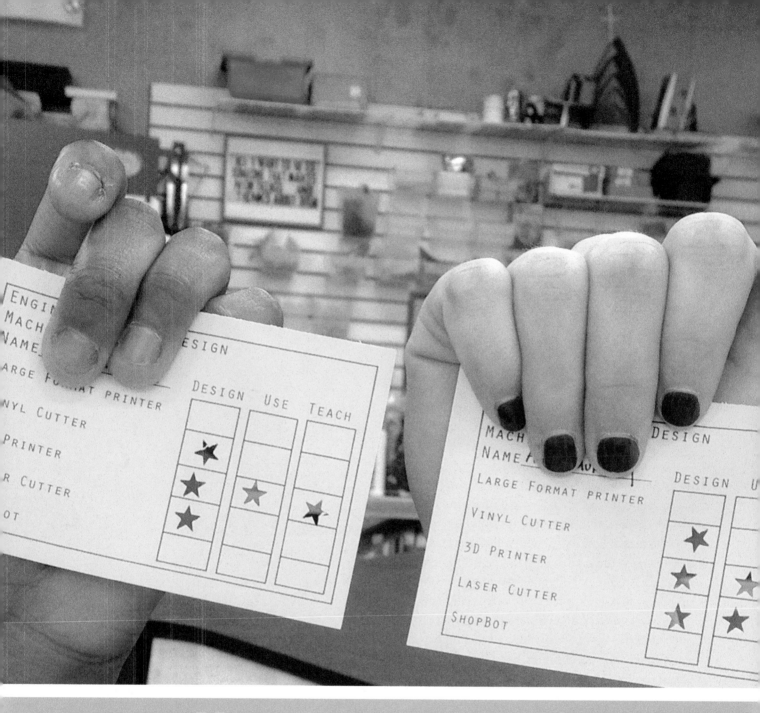

How Do We Know?
Assessment + Documentation

One of the most common questions about making in education revolves around assessment. How do you know what the students have learned? Can you prove it? Don't you have to give some sort of test to be sure? What if all the students are making different projects? What will I show my colleagues and administration as evidence of student achievement?

For educators launching a journey into a new kind of teaching and learning, answering these questions with certainty may seem like an impossible task. Yet many educators such as music or art teachers are able to evaluate student work even though students may be playing different instruments and painting different paintings. There is a long history and body of research supporting project-based learning and authentic assessment, yet many teachers have not been exposed to these techniques.

The articles in this section attempt to showcase the real ways that teachers are grappling with the questions of authentic assessment in today's classrooms.

Alternative Assessments and Feedback in a "Maker" Classroom

by Christa Flores

The rapid growth of "maker education" programs

According to Google Trends (fig. 9.1), the term *maker education*, or *makered* for short, came into existence around September 2004 and quickly became synonymous with progressive education and a resurgence of STEAM education in America. Although the exact number of what are now called "making in education" programs is not currently known, schools that employ a progressive pedagogy (or progressive *innovative* pedagogy for those working in the twenty-first century) or schools that make claims regarding the importance of differentiation, constructivism, or experiential learning have built or are building makerspaces and talking about maker education programs. At first these programs seemed to depend on having state-of-the-art makerspaces or fabrication labs (fab labs) stocked with high-tech tools, as most were found in well-funded private schools. That picture has changed rapidly in the past ten years, however, since the maker movement has gained popularity. More and more public and charter schools and nonprofit organizations are building programs that rival many private school makerspaces and fab labs. In fact, programs with limited budgets and space have reminded us that scarcity is an invaluable teacher in any good maker culture as it breeds creativity and self-reliance. Many of the maker education programs serving lower-income communities have access to mentors who never stopped working with their hands, even when it fell out of status in a consumer-driven America in the 1980s (Curtis and Kelsall 2002). While lower-income mentors may not know how to code in Python or what an Arduino microcomputer is, they are skilled carpenters, mechanics, seamstresses, and cooks and know what it means to be resourceful.

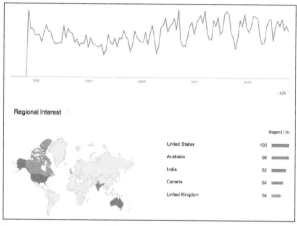

Figure 9.1: Google search history for "maker education." *Credit: Google Trends*

As with any progressive education discourse that seeks to reform the current education system in America, maker programs serving public schools are at the heart of this movement. Despite hope driven by the first-ever White House Maker Faire and President Obama's declaration of June 17, 2015, as the National Day of Making, most public schools still lack access to project- or problem-based programs. Those working in a maker education program know this kind of work/learning is good for kids as well as communities, and have the energy to fight to keep their programs alive. To support these teachers and to keep maker education programs sustainable, that is, to not let them suffer the fate of previous progressive education movements labeled as lacking rigor, we need to be thinking about the following ways assessments are used:

- By students for real learning
- By high schools and colleges for enrollment decisions
- By a community norm system to establish authority or job readiness (badge or certification system)
- To inform the efficacy of a maker program (research)

Defining assessment and feedback

Discussing assessment and feedback begins with having a conversation about learning in general. Whether an infant, an adult, or a Jack Russell terrier, learning happens every day and in a rich array of ways. Merriam Webster defines learning as "the activity or process of gaining knowledge or skill by studying, practicing, being taught, or experiencing something." Albert Einstein described learning as "when you are doing something with such enjoyment that you don't notice that the time passes."[1]

Whether you take the more "traditional school" description offered by Merriam Webster or the more blissful picture painted by Einstein, learning is a process. It is a process that can be intentional as when we make a conscious effort to learn Mandarin, or it can be unintended such as when "mistakes" take us down new and unexpected paths of discovery. For the purpose of this article, I will refer only to intentional learning, or events when the learner has a defined learning goal.

While learning is happening, assessment is the cognitive processing of outcomes in an attempt to reach a goal. Assessment is at first a snapshot to determine success or failure, then more deeply a survey of the factors that led to that success or failure. (If done methodically through documentation, this is science.) Feedback regarding an action is strongly tied to the physical environment as it reflects the result of the learner's action. Feedback is not only observed but also felt by the learner. Shame, pride, excitement, shock, etc., about the outcome (pass or fail) of actions drives the motivation to act again and again, learning through iteration.

Adapted from various learning models, including the Kolb model (fig. 9.2),[2] the diagram in figure 9.3 shows the growth pattern a learner follows when seeking to learn with an intended goal in mind (Kolb and Fry 1975). The goal may be to walk, make a soufflé, or pronounce a glottal stop. If the goal is reached, we call that a *pass*. If the goal is not reached, that can be called a *fail*. After the action takes place, the learner processes the outcome or consequences of his or her actions through two filters: the cognitive self and the emotional self. The cognitive self seeks to diagnose the reason for the failure or the success. (Diagnosing failure for avoidance, especially if pain was involved, can be easier than diagnosing a success for repetition.) The emotional self fills a vital role at this point. Classroom teachers call this emotional element of learning *engagement* or *motivation*. Studies in behavior and neuroscience have shown that emotional responses to success and failures, as long as a failure does not result in death, are key evolutionary tools driving learning (Arias-Carrión and Pöppel 2007).

When failure is tied to a student's actions and the student is the only one around to witness that failure (privacy to fail), learning occurs naturally and even blissfully. Learners must experience both aspects of assessment—the cognitive as well as the emotional—to move forward with intention, purpose, and passion toward their learning goal. If success comes too easily, a learner may give up on a task out of boredom. If the task proves too frustrating, the learner may abandon the learning goal, adopt a closed mindset, and label oneself as a failure. Finding the perfect balance, a term referred to by some as *funstration* and others as the *zone of proximal development*, is key.

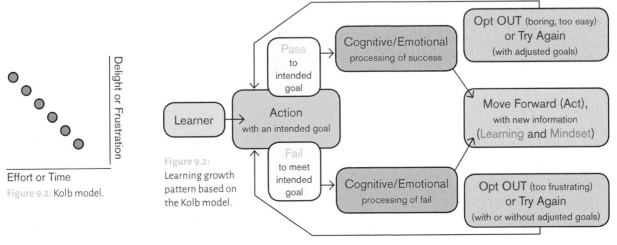

Delight or Frustration

Effort or Time

Figure 9.2: Kolb model.

Figure 9.2: Learning growth pattern based on the Kolb model.

Learner → Action with an intended goal

Pass to intended goal → Cognitive/Emotional processing of success → Opt OUT (boring, too easy) or Try Again (with adjusted goals)

Fail to meet intended goal → Cognitive/Emotional processing of fail → Opt OUT (too frustrating) or Try Again (with or without adjusted goals)

Move Forward (Act), with new information (Learning and Mindset)

Student- or teacher-driven learning and assessment

When a teacher is handed the responsibility for building the curriculum that students will be learning from September through June, this is considered a 100 percent teacher-driven learning environment. Often this style of education has preset assessment tools in the form of a test or rubric made well in advance of their need. In contrast, student-driven learning would entail students having a degree of choice in the content they will study, the skills they will be building, or the assessment used to illustrate their learning. Some combination of teacher- and student-centered learning is more likely the typical experience, but there are clear differences seen in public versus private school education settings.

In a traditional academic setting the teacher functions as the dark orange square in figure 9.3, the cognitive processing of a success or failure. As such, the teacher is entrusted with the wisdom, expertise, and fairness to assess each student's level of and potential for learning, at least in one discipline. When learners are removed from the critical assessment process in this way, they are left with how they feel about a success or failure but are not encouraged to take part in the empowering aspect of constructing the causal relationships between their actions and their successes or failures. Removing the cognitive from the emotional, for both learner and teacher, creates an imbalance that gives assessment in a rote-learning environment a bad name. As Dale Dougherty, founder of *Make:* magazine, said, "[Making] is intrinsic, whereas a lot of traditional, formal school is motivated by extrinsic measures, such as grades. Shifting that control from the teacher or the expert to the participant to the non-expert, the student, that's the real big difference here."[3]

In a maker classroom, learning is inherently experiential and can be very student driven; assessment and feedback need to look different than a paper test to accurately document and encourage learning. Regardless of how you feel about standardized testing, making seems to be immune to it for the time being (which is one reason some schools skip the assessment piece and offer mak-

ing as an extracurricular enrichment program). Encouragingly, the lack of any obvious right answers about how to measure and gauge success and failure in a maker classroom, as well as the ambiguity about how making in education fits into the common standards or college readiness debate, has not stopped schools from marching forward in creating their own maker programs.

Qualitative versus quantitative assessment and feedback

Grades are quantitative, discrete numbers, asked to be a standard language of achievement. Grades are by definition summative, or an inflexible snapshot of what a student knows and does not know at any point in time. Due to the nature of these discrete, universal numbers, they are used to rank children locally (within their classroom or community) as well as globally and have enjoyed the status of proof of rigor. Whether you are a ten-year-old in Santa Cruz, California, or a ten-year-old in Nairobi, Kenya, an A in math is supposed to mean something. In contrast, formative assessment is a vital element in the process of learning and is best left to qualitative tools such as oral feedback from peers and adults, narratives, and self-assessments. Unfortunately, formative assessments lack the status given to a letter grade. Although new methods for assessing meaningful work and learning through projects are emerging, such as maker portfolios being accepted at the Massachusetts Institute of Technology (MIT), for example, we are still working primarily within a grade-based system. As a result, any project can be graded using a clear set of concept- or skill-related goals in the form of a rubric.

In summary, giving a grade based on a paper test to measure achievement in STEAM still fails to compute in a maker education program, and other quantitative assessments may have a life span as well. Neuroscience and educational research assures us that qualitative feedback and self-assessment do more for passion-based learning then red marks on a test or high scores on standardized tests. The difference translates to mindsets, argues Mariale Hardiman, professor of education at the Johns Hopkins University School of Education and cofounder and director of the university's Neuro-Education Initiative. "As the research strongly suggests," states Hardiman, "when students focus on mastery of learning rather than on their performance on tests, they significantly increase their intrinsic motivation for learning" (Hardiman and Whitman 2014).

Facing assessment in public and private schools today

If we look closely at the pedagogical backbone of maker education, the lens would clearly reveal experiential learning and student-driven projects, which can be more challenging to assess, at their core. That being said, as paid professionals we need to adhere to a few constraints while we also strive to help kids be their best. Those two main constraints are standardized curriculum, as a result of an industrialized model of education, and current assumptions about college preparation and career readiness. Below is an examination of each as related to assessment in public and private PK–12 schools today.

Common Core

Described by the well intentioned as "a common set of rigorous national standards (that) will transform American education, prepare students for college and careers, and allow our nation to maintain international competitiveness," the Common Core is a set of educational benchmarks in math and literacy designed to be taught, then tested for proficiency by schools. Essentially the Common Core is a management strategy to hold schools accountable for their use of government funding. Resulting test scores on Common Core assessments determine how "well" a school is doing at educating America's children. In simpler terms, the Common Core ensures that schools with good test scores are given continued funding for a job well done.

A one-size-fits-all model to force accountability in public schools is an Orwellian and inelegant solution to a systemic failure of industrialized education. That said, it's the law of the land for most American children. We owe it to those children to disrupt the system with measurable evidence of how using a maker education program to teach math and literacy is better than using a one-size-fits-all curriculum that focuses on testing versus experiential learning.

College preparation versus life preparation

Just as the Common Core promises to maintain standards in the public school industry, college readiness is the number one claim made by most private schools. The problem is that college preparatory schools cannot guarantee that all of their clients get into top high schools or colleges; only the top-performing students will receive those slots, and thus the race begins. Assessment in this environment is driven by ranking students rather than focusing on learning and growth, something that can occur in a competitive environment for some but not others. Some outspoken educational reformers such as Ken Robinson are now arguing that college might get you a good unpaid internship but a well-paying career is not guaranteed. Prepping for life, on the other hand, according to Tony Wagner (2012), is about cultivating mindsets, especially those that support creative problem solving and entrepreneurialism for a rapidly changing global economy.

Regardless of well-intentioned educational reform debates, powerful systems of status quo in the higher education realm still trickle all the way down to prekindergarten pedagogy in ways that make one cringe. *College readiness* has become synonymous with stressed out, competitive, overbooked youth that struggle with autonomy and are more "at risk" than their lower-income counterparts. It's not good for kids, and it's not good for family dynamics. Assessments used by admissions that support the current status quo in college readiness, good or bad, set the standards for the rest of the independent school industry. Teachers that fall into this category need evidence that making is important for college readiness, as that definition currently stands, in ways that rival standardized test scores. Research and collaboration around best practice for switching from test-based assessments to alternative systems, such as portfolios, is a vital component to keeping maker education programs sustainable.

Making is "just" arts and crafts with a technology twist—it is not rigorous enough

Using pedagogical practices that fall under the title of "making" are subject to the discourse around how to ensure and measure rigor. The usual answer to the problem of rigor (which is code for *college readiness*) is to have standardized tests. Tests are reassuring data points that allow administration and parents and admissions officers to feel like we are basing policy on logical and scientific measures. This is where progressive education loses the fight. No matter how student centered or innovative your curriculum, giving a letter grade to students at the end of a course, focuses attention (and attention is what we value) on product over process. This imbalance in priorities is beginning to not only confuse constructivist educators but parents as well. Three events described below caused me to again reflect on assessment and how it plays a vital and controversial role in making in educational settings.

The first event was a conversation between two of my students, who spoke on the student panel at the FabLearn 2014 conference, and audience member and FabLearn Fellow colleague Jaymes Dec. When Jaymes asked my students at the end of their talk how they were graded, there was a pregnant pause. It was at that moment I realized that they did not have a clear idea of how they were "tested" on their project. Then one said with some reservation, "We were graded on how we got along." The second student added with a bit more assurance, "We were also graded on a Pass or Fail. If we got the machine to work, we passed. If we didn't, we failed."

In reality, I graded them on a point system likened to the Pass/Fail concept but with room for random point loss to make the system look normal. They earned points for their work away from school (homework points), and they got points for meeting benchmarks (reflections on peer critique sessions) as well as turning in video or written essays (self-assessments) defending a grade of Pass or Fail. In the end I am assessing how well they can make a claim, support it with evidence, and tell the most accurate and compelling story of their education. I am training them to think like

scientists and to speak like storytellers. Part of me feels a sense of relief that they don't know what part of their year gets the final grade. That way they see all the parts as potentially important, not just the behaviors that can affect their letter grade.

The second event was another conversation—this one, with two very intelligent people—about the style of assessment I have been testing and using for the past two years in a making-centered classroom at Hillbrook School in Los Gatos, California. It also happened that the conversation was centered around a narrative report I had written regarding their son. In short, I found myself defending how I am able to whittle down all of the learning that happens in a unit that consists of single projects that can last two to four months out of a nine-month school year. That is a lot of schools hours to defend to a parent paying a premium for those hours. Unfortunately I do not have test scores on which to rest my claims. The assessment my students experience on a daily basis is formative in nature, ongoing, and extends outside the boundaries of a classroom. It cannot wait for the end of a unit; it must be happening at every moment.

Formative assessment that does not get a letter grade also allows students to feel assessed more on their collaboration skills, resilience, and ability to gain the knowledge necessary to improve the performance of their inventions—what they think is also important to be learning at their age.

The third event that sparked my imagination was listening to all of the dedicated and intelligent offerings at the FabLearn 2014 conference, which emphasized inclusivity and equity. I learned that making is artistic and about craftsmanship, so it is definitely arts and crafts, but that is just semantics. Making is also about gaining mathematical literacy through doing and testing. It is about asking questions and collecting information like a real scientist. Making is also transforming kids' experiences of school by teaching them how to think, and giving them a sense of purpose and competence that can lead to a lifelong love of learning and problem solving.

Finally, FabLearn 2014 opening keynote speaker Paula Hooper, senior science educator and learning research scientist at the Exploratorium, reminded us how constructivism fosters a sense of equity and inclusion for kids. Hooper told us a story of identity through agency and technology literacy. "You bring who you are culturally and the experiences of your past. Knowledge—that is not just connected to the mathematical concepts at hand," Hooper inspires us to dwell on. Making is an outlet for kids to be confident in math, science, and technology when they might have felt shut out in a more traditional science and math classroom. Add in the literacy skills needed to tell that rich of a learning journey and you are talking about one of the more engaging, not to mention authentically rigorous, curricula a school can provide for its students.

Notes

1. openculture.com/2015/05/einstein-tells-his-son-the-key-to-learning-happiness-is-losing-yourself-in-creativity.html
2. learningfromexperience.com/
3. ted.com/talks/dale_dougherty_we_are_makers

References

Arias-Carrión, Ó., & Pöppel, E. (2007). Dopamine, learning, and reward-seeking behavior. *Acta Neurobiologiae Experimentalis*, 67(4), 481–488.

Barseghian, T. (2014, July 9). A school that ditches all the rules, but not the rigor. [Blog post]. MindShift, KQED.org. Retrieved from kqed.org/mindshift/2014/07/09/a-school-that-ditches-all-the-rules-but-not-the-rigor-game-based-school-playmaker/

Borovoy, A. E., & Cronin, A. (2013, July). Resources for understanding the Common Core State Standards. *Edutopia*. Retrieved from edutopia.org/common-core-state-standards-resources

Costanza, K. (2013, September 17). The maker movement finds its way into urban classrooms. [Blog post]. *Mind/Shift*, KQED.org.

Curtis, A., & Kelsall, L. (Producers). (2002). The century of the self [Video]. Available from https://freedocumentaries.org/documentary/bbc-the-century-of-the-self-happiness-machines-season-1-episode-1

Hardiman, M., & Whitman, G. (2014, Winter). Assessment and the learning brain: What the research tells us. *Independent Magazine*. Retrieved from nais.org/Magazines-Newsletters/ISMagazine/Pages/Assessment-and-the-Learning-Brain.aspx

Kolb, D. A., & Fry, R. (1975). Toward an applied theory of experiential learning. In C. Cooper (Ed.), *Theories of group process*. London, UK: John Wiley.

Obama, B. (2014, June 17). Presidential Proclamation on National Day of Making.

Wagner, T. (2012). *Creating innovators: The making of young people who will change the world*. New York: Scribner.

10 Watching Children Learn

by Tracy Rudzitis

One of the most meaningful things that I get to do as a teacher is to watch students learn. What makes it most exciting and interesting for me is observing this learning through their eyes and their contexts. I have several Flip Video cameras located in the classroom along with my point-and-shoot camera, and the students ask me, "Where is the camera?" and "Can we use the camera?" or "We just did something really cool. Can we record it?"

One big project in the STEAM Lab at The Computer School (MS 245) in New York City[1] was the construction of Rube Goldberg machines (fig. 10.1). Students were grouped in teams of five—not the optimum size perhaps, but based on the reality of six tables and thirty students per class, eleven classes in total. You can imagine the amount of activity and experiences happening during any one moment of the fifty-minute class period—often too much for a single person to be able to observe, comment on, and monitor as well as explain, assist, find materials for, and prompt groups when they get "stuck." Having cameras that students can pick up and use at any point in the class gives me a window into the students' work that I might otherwise miss.

Each project includes a documentation component. The cameras provide a seamless way for students to document and think about what they are doing. Getting students to document their learning and their exploration of materials, concepts, and ideas can be a difficult task. Using design journals or handouts to encourage students to write and plan is one approach. Planning is an important part of the process, but students (and many times adults) are often impatient and want to start the project without spending too much time on the "thinking about it first" portion, which can take on the characteristics of school

Figure 10.1: Rube Goldberg or chain-reaction machine.

that are a challenge to many students. Sitting still with a blank sheet of paper and pencil on the desk, an outline of requirements on the board, and mind racing with the typical things that occupy a middle school student's mind are all in conflict with each other.

There has to be a space where the planning, thinking, design, making, experimenting, testing, reflection, and iteration can exist in harmony and equal passion. It is also important that the teacher be able to get a glimpse of the thinking and ideas that each student is contemplating while working through a project. Using video and photography provides an additional format for students.

Reviewing the photographs that the students make while documenting their work allows for a different insight into their thinking and their ideas. When you give sixth and seventh graders a reflection or a worksheet, the expectation is that the teacher provides the questions or prompts. The adult in the room has decided what is most worthy of discussion, what learning is to be addressed, what questions should be answered. When looking at the projects through the eyes of our students, we discover what they think is important, what they are discovering, what is new and exciting for them. We also get to see the focus and concentration in their approach to the work that is often captured unexpectedly or in spite of the enthusiasm that is also displayed. My students know the cameras are available at any time, and they understand the basic expectations: they are documenting their work, their process, their ideas. They know to pass the camera on to the next team when they are done, and not to worry about editing or viewing the photos until they are uploaded to the Google photo album.

Photographs can tell one part of the story; video can tell another. With the addition of a sound track or voice-over, the students can explain their work and speak about the process and what they have discovered. It offers insight into the project and can also address some of the more formal learning targets that the teacher might have for the students and the project.

The documentation of student work can provide significant evidence of student learning and understanding. Yet there is enormous tension between the predefined expectations often outlined in the rubrics and "students will be able "to . . ."" messages that are more often written for administrators than for students. Looking at student work is a process that is worthy of exploration, and there are several formal methods or protocols that can be used when looking at student work.[2] My ongoing quest is to measure student understanding in ways that are embedded and natural to the hands-on, constructivist learning environment.

Notes

1. sites.google.com/a/thecomputerschool.org /steam-cs/
2. lasw.org/methods.html

11 Documenting a Project Using a "Failures Box"

by Susanna Tesconi

At LABoral Centro de Arte y Creación Industrial in Gijón, Spain, groups from primary school to high school each work on a different project. Consequently a lot of prototypes are hanging around the Fab Lab. In order to keep the lab from getting too messy, each group fabricates stackable boxes by modifying a design from Thingiverse.[1] Modifying and fabricating the box is the first group activity, so it also serves as an introduction to laser and vinyl cutting.

After each session the kids put the items they make into the boxes (depending on the dimensions). The project/prototype "has permission" to stay out of the box only when the kids consider it shareable. When we get to that stage, I ask them to empty the box and reconstruct the evolution of the project by using the previous prototypes/failures as "chapters." They can make photos, videos, write text, dramatize, dance, etc., in order to explain what they did and how they feel about each step.

Generally they have a great time doing it, and they understand the importance of documenting in order to tell someone how to do something. And in doing so, they became aware of what they have learned. They laugh a lot about the previous failures and dead-end solutions. They seem more comfortable about previous feelings of frustration. It makes them more motivated to "own" their own projects and take risks.

Documenting something one made in order to share it is one of the most constructive practices of the maker culture. Thanks to documentation, people all around the world can learn, experiment, remix, and redesign, building on the base of other people's work. Knowledge sharing as the action of feeding a global shared brain makes all of us smarter and wiser.

During an inspiring conversation about hands-on learning activities, FabLearn Fellow Susan Klimczak told me, "In experiential learning, you know exactly what you have learned when you document it." Documentation is the missing ingredient in traditional thinking about assessment and self-learning. Many teachers involved in maker programs and schools are familiar with the idea of documentation as a base for assessment and formative (pedagogical) evaluation, but we can take advantage of the benefits of documentation in more ways.

We need to integrate documenting practices as part of making activities as well as designing, tinkering, digital fabrication, and programming in order to enable students to document their own learning process and experiment with the beauty of building shared knowledge. Documentation is a hard task even for adults, but it is not so hard if you design a reason and a consistent expectation that everyone will collect and organize the things they will share. This expectation of students contributing to the failure box is that it will help them tell the story of their project chapter by chapter.

Note

1. thingiverse.com/thing:3187

The Role of Peer Assessment in a Maker Classroom

by Christa Flores

Background

When I first started using a problem-based curriculum in science, I had no idea what to expect. Moreover, I had only a vague idea of how I was going to assess my students. As an academic teacher, I am required to give students a letter grade twice a year. While I am moving more strongly toward the use of portfolios and self-assessment in my classes, I still work within a system that strives to have letter grades accurately reflect a student's level of understanding or effort in a discipline, in my case fifth- and sixth-grade science. I work within a system (preschool through graduate school) that still values grades as an indicator of how to rank children. Ideally this ranking is used so they can be better served, classified, and counseled toward the goal of attending college and possibly future career choices. In this system, the easy-to-mass-produce-and-analyze discrete quality offered by tests makes for a more valued form of assessment. As a result, 5 percent of the letter grade is still the result of paper-style tests and quizzes, or what I refer to as "check-ins."

Beginning with the role of peer assessment, below I describe the role of alternative forms of assessment (the other 95 percent) that I have been using in my problem-based approach to science. The other forms of assessment that I use include self-assessment and assessment by a mentor or adult expert. A fourth form of assessment, one to which I was first introduced by Dave Otten of the Athenian School in Danville, California, is the role of authentic assessment in the form of published, or open-source, sharing of work. These forms of assessment may be used in conjunction with assigning letter grades, as any are easily adaptable to a rubric, or they can be used in a less-formal, gradeless setting. Regardless, they stand alone

in value as they bring a rare opportunity for the following student résumé to evolve over time:

- Leadership—through setting higher-quality standards of how to do work, the presentation of work, and risk taking by taking on hard problems
- Collaboration—through the sharing of ideas and constructive criticism
- The ability to defend an argument
- The ability to describe a problem
- Self-awareness as a learner
- Practicing informed iteration while working toward a solution

Why peer assessment?

Forgetting for a minute that my students are ages ten and eleven (as I must to begin to learn their strengths), I researched forms of assessment, seeking out assessment that would be most authentic to a maker classroom. For me, that looked like behaviors (assessment tools) that led to methods (feedback) for offering new ideas, and collaboration on the growth process of designing a product. Although I felt that peer critique was aligned with the previously stated goals, I had no measure to back up my claim. My fear of the blind leading the blind over a cliff of failure existed at the beginning of the year, as it would for most teachers. But peer review is crucial in science, and it works in various design fields, so why not in a classroom? Using peer critique to give rapid feedback on the design process seemed better than trying to filter all student work through the lens of one teacher. Peer feedback was not only useful but necessary in an open-ended project scenario.

Having taught middle school for fourteen years, I also knew that the role of peer opinion, as it affects some beliefs and some behaviors, begins to supersede the role of parents and other adults at this developmental age (Berndt 1979). Lastly, due to the democratic nature in which knowledge will be accessed in this century, as well as our school's location in the heart of the technology world of Silicon Valley, many students come to the classroom with valuable insights, experiences, and opinions that could inform the whole group. Why not capitalize on these assets?

In the end, the blind leading the blind is often how we all embark on an adventure. Every year we have to learn as a class or team how to critique the work of others by doing it a few times. It takes modeling comments and questions in the first few attempts at peer critique to get students to make more thoughtful and insightful criticisms of their classmates' work. Over time students, too, will inform the group as to what "quality" looks like. The quality of observations being made by the audience also increases over time. This, in turn, leads to a higher quality of feedback for the presenter. Presentation styles can also be informed through critiquing the quality of a presentation.

Students soon learn from each other two key elements of sharing their work: the importance of a "good story" about their work, and that data visualization is worth a thousand words.

Formal versus informal critiques

Students can earn feedback from their peers in two different ways in class—formally and informally. When we first began the year, all presentations of work for peer feedback were given formally, that is, one or two students giving a slideshow-aided presentation of the current progress of their work (fig. 12.1). These formal "crits" (as students call them) were modeled on

Figure 12.1: Formal student presentations.

the first year we used product design in the sixth-grade curriculum (Flores 2013). I soon noticed that the quality of peer feedback grew over several weeks, and I began to trust my students to give key feedback that I would have been dishing out as the adult in the room. With that role covered by my most ardent student critics, I now reserve my comments to offer clues to a solution or for direct suggestions to deepen their knowledge, as any literacy guru would do.

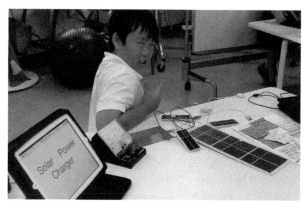

Figure 12.2: Student-led informal design critiques.

The problem with formal critiques is that they are formal. Many adolescents hate public speaking, and they take many days out of class time to do properly (time for both presentations and feedback). That is a lot to sit through, no matter how interesting it may be. To add to that, the process of active listening for critical feedback is exhausting. I have to remind myself often, that these students are only eleven. We brainstormed as a class ways to improve the system, and two ideas emerged. Students almost unanimously agreed that peer critiques were valuable. Rather than have every share of work be done formally, they decided to do informal style critiquing, where students share their work more science-fair style. For informal critiques, several tables are set up gallery style throughout the iLab. Students can then design their work display using whiteboard tables (fig. 12.2), rolling white boards, markers, standing their iPads up as displays, and displaying their prototypes in an analog timeline (fig. 12.3).

The second idea to make formal crits less painful came when we needed to participate in a series of formal critiques for students to share the results of their product development testing. This critique needed to be formal as students presented

Figure 12.3: A timeline of prototypes.

their authentic questions about their work to this point. To help get through the process more easily and effectively, we made sure to schedule only five presentations a day over a series of days, and always indulged in an intermission that required no brain cells (any YouTube video with kittens getting stuck in things will do). The key was to keep the learning process fun, even if it was still formal.

Feedback

As peers take in the description of work from those presenting, they know that a valuable part of the process is to give real criticism to the presenter. This feedback can be verbal and interactive, such as that given at the end of a formal presentation of work, or it can be more passive; feedback in the form of what we call "love notes," or sticky notes and sharpie markers (fig. 12.4). These brightly colored love notes can have an effect on a student's project on different layers—emotional as well as cognitive. The sheer act of getting a paper covered in love notes still brings a bright-eyed glow of relief to the face of a student having survived a presentation. The students seem to genuinely

Figure 12.4: Students leaving "love notes" for their peers using the sticky note and Sharpie model.

feel rewarded for their intellect and work by the simplest of notes such as those scribbled with the words "Very cool!" or "I liked your ideas." What adult wouldn't want to get that kind of encouragement for their work on a regular basis? The key to using peers to critique student work is that feedback is immediate and expected by the student presenters, which can be a very powerful motivator to do well (Kettle and Häubl 2010).

Love notes can offer key steps to academic growth as well. As research into effective peer assessment for massive open online courses (MOOCs) has shown, peer assessment can be as effective as assessment done by a single adult or teacher (Koller 2012; Sadler and Good 2006). While a maker classroom is not a MOOC, it is a place where student-driven work can seem overwhelming for a single teacher to assess. Using peer assessment allows for deeper differentiation in the learning process for students, something we strive for at Hillbrook School (Los Gatos, California).

One student's scientific question was whether she could prevent bananas from turning brown in her ice-cream recipe. Her ice cream was designed to combat depression, the problem she chose to investigate for the year. Once she decided to make a food-related solution, she researched micronutrients that aid in the relief of depression and invented an ice cream.

Can we measure the value of peer critique?

It is one thing to have an intuition that something is valuable in your classroom. It is another to be able to share something of value outside of your classroom using only anecdotal evidence. Isolated in the iLab, I could see growth happening in the students due to the peer critique system we had been using. Still, I struggled with a method of measuring the value so that I could explain the value to others. After deliberation with Hillbrook School's science teacher and Center for Teaching Excellence research design guru Ilsa Dohman, I began asking students to reflect on the peer critique process. I asked them to dwell on the process while they focused on the following topics:

1. Determining the goal of this presentation of your work

2. Self-assessing your presentation in terms of quality

3. Tweezing out constructive criticism from the love notes to decide on a plan of action for your next iteration

Can students keep better track of how the comments and feedback they get from their peers is reflected in their iteration process or growth as a student? If so, we can all see the value of the process.

References

Berndt, T. J. (1979). Developmental changes in conformity to peers and parents. *Developmental Psychology, 15*(6), 608–616. doi: 10.1037/0012 -1649.15.6.608

Boundless. (n.d.). Peer groups. Boundless.com. Retrieved from boundless.com/sociology /textbooks/boundless-sociology-textbook /socialization-4/agents-of-socialization-46 /peer-groups-285-9603/

Flores, C. (2013). Authentic learning and assessment in the self-directed environment of a middle school maker space. Paper presented at IDC 2013—Interaction Design and Children Conference.

Kettle, K., & Häubl, G. (2010). Motivation by anticipation: Expecting rapid feedback enhances performance. *Psychological Science 21*(4), 545–547.

Koller, D. (2012, June). What we're learning from online education. [Video.] TEDGlobal. Available from ted.com/talks/daphne_koller _what_we_re_learning_from_online _education?language=en

Sadler, P. M., & Good, E. (2006). The impact of self- and peer-grading on student learning. *Educational Assessment, 11*(1), 1–31.

Senger, J. L., & Kanthan, R. (2012). Student evaluations: Synchronous tripod of learning portfolio assessment—Self-assessment, peer-assessment, instructor-assessment. *Creative Education, 3*(1), 155–163.

The Role and Rigor of Self-Assessment in Maker Education

by Christa Flores

What is self-assessment?

The purpose of teacher-driven assessment is to measure whether a student is ready to move on to the next topic in a given curriculum. Often this translates to the next chapter of a textbook. If the student passes the teacher's assessment, the next step in her education is given to her in lockstep manner. This approach to learning and assessment, while comfortably quantifiable, unfortunately fails to approach the full spectrum of learning that modern-day education has to offer children and adults. Throw makerspaces into the mix, and you have a recipe for a revolution in assessment, beginning with handing the right and responsibility of assessment over to our students.

Dr. Betty McDonald, manager of the Professional Development Unit, The Learning Centre at University of Trinidad and Tobago, and leader in the field of using self-assessment to support individualization, describes self-assessment in the following manner: "the involvement of students in identifying standards and/or criteria to apply to their work and making judgments about the extent to which they have met these criteria and standards." When a learner does not utilize the insight of others more than their own critical insight into their progress toward a learning goal, they are using self-assessment. *Self-assessment* is any form of assessment that is undertaken by the learner as a first person. Autonomy to diagnose one's work (with or without the aid of an expert) can come into play cyclically during a making activity. Documenting that process becomes, by necessity, the responsibility of the learner.

What are the nuts and bolts of self-assessment? Regardless of how you define it, using self-assessment allows a learner to work toward an ability to accomplish the following:

Critique quality of work (self and others)
- Based on principles of design, science, engineering, and research
- Based on a rubric of preselected standards created by students or teacher
- Based on peer feedback and classroom mentoring

Diagnose and describe a problem/propose solutions
- Documentation, verbal or written, of pass or fail for a given goal (can be 100 percent teacher or student driven)

Communicate competence and reasoning
- Illustrate knowledge of concepts or skills through application (authentic assessments such as Pass/Fail) or representation (as in a paper test or essay)
- Argue for the use of specific materials and design ideas
- Mentor others in the use of a tool or technique

Relevance

Need to know how to clean a carburetor, make a soufflé, or pronounce Dutch words? Students can instantly explore any topic or new skill they are passionate about by browsing YouTube or any other DIY site. Awareness that education, or learning in general, will no longer be the proprietary interest of a few elite institutions, Raymond Cirmo of Cheshire Academy in Connecticut and vice president of the Connecticut Science Teachers Association sums up this inevitable shift from teacher-driven curriculum to student driven when he says, "We first need to realize that the students are not in our classroom; we are in their classroom. And the room is not set up for us to teach; it is there for us to be facilitators in the students' learning" (2014). Combine access with motivation and you have an increasingly self-educated population led by experts and amateurs alike.

With trends toward more differentiation in education, also termed a *student-centered* approach to learning, the teacher no longer defines, or impedes, what students find relevant or engaging to learn. Gary Stager, coauthor of *Invent to Learn: Making, Tinkering, and Engineering in the Classroom* and the founder of the Constructing Modern Knowledge summer educator institute, advocates the following mantra: "Less us, more them." This tactic may work well for encouraging a love of learning, but what happens when you are part of a system that gives students grades?

In the more self-directed learning environments of making in education, content knowledge is gained as it becomes relevant to a solution for a problem at hand. Not every student learns the same concepts or acquires the same skills. This presents a major problem for assessing a student on a standardized scale. Consider the alternative: teaching content to assess the retention of content as the Common Core has left many doing. Assuming you agree, that we are heading in the correct direction in education, you may then wonder, "Where does all of this relinquishing of power leave us as teachers? What active role do we take as the champions of our students' passions and pursuits of purpose?"

I believe that making-in-education practitioners and champions will offer the best classroom models to answer these questions. Witnessing the wonders of making in education teaches us to foster an environment of growth and self-actualization by using forms of assessment that challenge our students to critique both their own work and the work of their peers. This is where the role of self-assessment begins to shine a light.

What we gain from self-assessment

Shifting assessment in the classroom from the hands of the adult educator to the empowered learner can include the following educational benefits:

- **Assessment literacy.** Students learn how to critique their own work and the work of others for quality, growth, and even creativity.
- **Communicators who defend a claim.** Students learn to use argument, logic, evidence-based reasoning, and various literacy (including technology) skills to judge and defend a claim about their work. Students practice making thinking visible.[1]
- **Twenty-first century librarians.** Our students are growing up in a world where information is increasingly free and accessible to those with Internet access. The ability to navigate one's own learning using the sea of available resources is a vital skill to be cultivated.
- **Participation in democratic education.** Allowing students to have a say in what they learn as well as how they share, celebrate, and give evidence of growth allows for a more empowered learner.

In summary, using nontraditional forms of assessment to support students can feel risky and messy. Keep faith, however, as Dr. Betty MacDonald of the University of Trinidad and Tobago noted: "The process is time consuming, but the dividends are worth far more than the time invested, especially when you consider the long-term benefits of life-long learning" (2012c).

How effective is self-assessment?

Giving a student a rubric and asking him to grade himself is a form of self-assessment. Expecting that student to be honest (after all, grades can be high stakes) or to understand the rubric created by another person brings to question not only the accuracy of this assessment tool but also the time payoff, especially when compared to quicker or traditional forms of assessment. While rubrics are helpful and make the self-grading process appear more democratic, when not cocreated with the student, rubrics may include inherent bias or erred perceptions of understanding. Studies at Stanford in 2001 about self-assessment tools in medical school confirmed that students were inaccurate at assessing their level of knowledge on a given subject (Dunning, Heath, and Suls 2004).

Stories and studies that paint a positive light on self-assessment[2] argue that the focus of these assessments should be formative to avoid issues of disenfranchisement or inaccuracy (Andrade and Valtcheva 2009). Formative assessment is process versus product centered as well as more authentic, or embedded into a student's learning.[3] As such, formative assessments foster a growth mindset and a safe space to give and hear critical feedback. The message of a formative assessment is that "we are all still learning." Examples of formative assessments can be design or engineering logs that record diagnosis and design ideas, maker portfolios,[4] or informal work shares for peer feedback.[5]

Because formative assessment happens more than just at the end of a chapter or unit, it can be seen as too time-consuming. The time used to do these assessments, some will argue, is a vital part of the learning and offers a deeper more holistic payoff compared to the quicker standardized test (McDonald 2012a). Furthermore, self-assessment was found to make students smarter and more motivated according to a 2012 study by Dr. Betty McDonald. She found that "students of the experimental group (those who used self-assessment) were able to pinpoint their specific areas for improvement whilst those of the control group took no interest in determining ways for improvement" (2012b).

Thankfully self-assessment does not have to be based on content knowledge, nor does it have to be done in a vacuum to be effective. Developing assessment literacy does seem to be key to successful self- and peer-assessment, however (Smith et al. 2011). Combining forms of peer-assessment with self-assessments can help students gain this vital assessment literacy.

In an *Edutopia* article from 1997, Clyde Yoshida, a seventh- and eighth-grade math teacher using a design-based math project, describes assessment literacy as follows: "We want (students) to be able to judge for themselves whether a piece of work is excellent or falls short of the school's standards. It may seem like a lot to ask of adolescents, but once we started using strategies such as critique circles and portfolios, students quickly showed they were willing and able to take more responsibility for the quality of their work."

This idea of assessment literacy or quality, as relevant to one's own education and experiences, is one that took time for me to trust, especially after reading *Zen and the Art of Motorcycle Maintenance*, which dissects the idea of quality *ad nauseum*. In the end, once I realized quality was relative, collaborative, and constructivist,[6] I began to trust the process much more. Now, I ask students to pick out works of quality and attempt to define the terms for themselves.

The following three ideas seem to point toward effective self-assessment:

1. Using self-assessment to reach a letter grade that is more summative in nature versus formative[7] can lead to inaccuracies, defeat the goal of the assessment, and give alternative assessments a bad name. Assessment needs to feel safe for students, and that is possible when you practice a growth or "maker" mindset[8] around work and assessment.

2. Self-assessment can facilitate deeper learning as it requires students to play a more active role in the cause of their success and failures as well as practice a critical look at quality.

3. The role of peers and the sharing of work leads to a community-wide assessment literacy that increases the accuracy of self-assessment as well as the rewards of using alternative assessments.

The efficacy of self-assessment as well as return for time spent is reliant on two factors. First, we must create a safe space for self- and peer critique to occur by promoting process over product and a growth mindset. Second, we must collaboratively build assessment literacy. As with any kind of literacy, assessment literacy takes time and gets better with modeling and practice. Deeply dependent on collaboration and communication with peers, practicing assessment literacy together leads to more effective assessments as well as a more democratic and engaging learning environment.

Notes

1. youtube.com/watch?v=AQTYcZf40ag
2. edutopia.org/blog/self-assessment -inspires-learning-lori-desautels
3. youtube.com/watch?v=WusyF6hRMRs#t=95
4. fablearn.stanford.edu/fellows/blog/maker -portfolios-authentic-assessment-tells-story
5. youtube.com/watch?v=60mXFeuhwfw
6. youtube.com/watch?v=hqh1MRWZjms
7. cmu.edu/teaching/assessment/basics /formative-summative.html
8. usergeneratededucation.wordpress.com /2014/10/08/the-mindset-of-the -maker-educator/

References

Andrade, H., & Valtcheva, A. (2009). Promoting learning and achievement through self-assessment. *Theory into Practice*, 48(1), 12–19.

Cirmo, R. W. (2014, Winter). Getting our students to own their educational experience. *Independent School*. Retrieved from nais.org/Magazines-Newsletters /ISMagazine/Pages/Getting-Our -Students-to-Own-Their-Educational -Experience.aspx

Dunning, D., Heath, C., & Suls, J. M. (2004). *Flawed self-assessment: Implications for health, education, and the workplace*. Malden, MA: Blackwell Publishers.

McDonald, B. (2012a). Gestalt effect of self-assessment. Retrieved from files.eric.ed.gov/fulltext /ED538072.pdf

McDonald, B. (2012b). Self assessment and student centred learning. Retrieved from researchgate.net/publication/265057406 _McDonald_B_2012c_Self_Assessment_and _Student_Centred_Learning_Retrieved_from _ERIC_database_ED_536980

McDonald, B. (2012c). Using self-assessment to support individualized learning. *Mathematics Teaching*, 231, 26–27.

Pahomov, L. (2014, December 3). What meaningful reflection on student work can do for learning. *MindShift*. Retrieved from kqed.org /mindshift/2014/12/03/what-meaningful -reflection-on-student-work-can-do-for-learning/

Pirsig, R. M. (1974). *Zen and the art of motorcycle maintenance: An inquiry into values*. New York, NY: Morrow.

Smith, C. D., Worsfold, K., Davies, L., Fisher, R., & McPhail, R. (2013). Assessment literacy and student learning: The case for explicitly developing students "assessment literacy." *Assessment & Evaluation in Higher Education*, 38(1), 44–60.

Stager, G. S. (n.d.). Less us, more them. [Blog post]. Retrieved from http://stager.tv /blog/?p=2358

Yoshida, C. (1997, July 1). Creating a culture of student reflection: Self-assessment yields positive results. *Edutopia*. Retrieved from edutopia.org /creating-culture-student-reflection

14 Examples of Self-Assessment in Making in Education

by **Christa Flores and Carolina Rodriguez**

In this article we will look at how to use self-assessment in a real-world project context.

Example self-assessment tool 1: Student surveys

Sixth-Grade Project 2014: School of the Future
School: Downtown College Prep (San Jose, California)
Curriculum Designer: Nina Rodriguez

Eight sixth graders at Downtown College Prep met in the Innovation and Design Lab two days out of the week for one hour after school. The sixth graders met a total of eight sessions to work on the School of the Future project, which consisted of student teams responsible for designing a specific type of building (e.g., the library, the multipurpose room, the front office) for a brand-new campus. The goal for each team was to create a design that demonstrated empathy toward the needs of the staff and students who would use the facility as well as to make a unique structure that reflected their own idea of what a school of the future would look like. Prior to starting the program, students filled out a questionnaire with the following questions:

- Why do you want to participate in the School of the Future project?
- What do you hope to learn at this after-school program?
- Have you ever made a model of a building? If you have, what did you build?

When reading the completed surveys, it was clear that they had a strong interest in making as well as a familiarity with the very basics of the design process. The goal was to use this knowledge that they already had to help them determine which aspect of the project they wanted to learn more about. These questions served as an introductory self-assessment for the students, in the sense that they were describing their own motivations for taking the time to work on this project outside of school as well as their expectations for their own learning.

Student attitudes

At the beginning of the School of the Future project the students completed a presurvey (fig. 14.1), and they completed a postsurvey at the end to track their changing attitudes (fig. 14.2). The students' responses demonstrated that self-

---

Why do you want to participate in the School of the Future project?

- "Because I want to make new things and to try new things."
- "Because I really like to build stuff."
- "Because one day I can do something and change the world."
- "I want to participate in the School of the Future project because it's a creative group and I like to do creative things like: drawing, inventing, etc."

What do you hope to learn at this after-school program?

- "More about science and designing stuff."
- "How to do step by step things to get to one big thing."
- "How to express myself by being more creative."
- "I hope to learn more [about] how to invent things."

Have you ever made a model of a building? If you have, what did you build?

"I made a model out of pipe cleaners at school with Jasmine and Juan. We made something that looks like the [Eiffel] tower."

Figure 14.1: Student presurvey.

Student Feedback: School of the Future Survey

What was your favorite step in the design process?

- "My favorite part of the design was the putting together part."
- "My favorite step was working together."
- "My favorite step was ideate because I got to brainstorm different things."
- "The building part where we made the models."

What did you learn from working on this project?

- "I learned to express my ideas and present in front of a lot of people."
- "I learned that there are a lot of steps in the design process."
- "What I learned from working on the project was to build many things you have ideas on."
- "I learned about measuring and which materials works."

What would you have liked to learn more about?

- "I would have liked to learn more about different designs for the building."
- "Building big things like a tower."
- "Painting"
- "Maybe how many people it took to make a building."
- "How people would like to rate it."

Figure 14.2: Student postsurvey.

assessment helps them discover specific interests as compared to when they first started the project. Having a prompt with parameters definitely focuses their attention on certain skills, but when the magnifying glass placed over their work is through the students' eyes, they become active rather than passive learners.

In the presurvey, students described what they wanted to do ("make stuff," "drawing," inventing"), while in the reflection survey, they start to focus on achievements and challenges throughout their design process for their project, such as presenting their work at the school assembly or learning how to determine what materials worked best for their models. In addition, the students also made direct connections to the design process (fig. 14.3) when reflecting on their learning experience, which was the primary focus for the project.

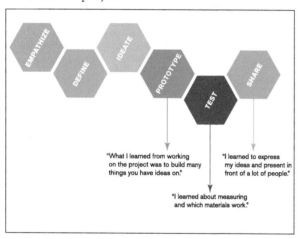

Figure 14.3: Student connections to the design process.
Credit: IDEAco, CityX Project

These students have shown that they can express their expectations for their learning experience as well as recognize the primary concept(s) of a project. Surveys can be used as a starting point for in-depth self-assessment and can also be incorporated to help students when they are struggling to discern the successful aspects of their work as well as the components of the project they need to improve or address.

Example self-assessment tool 2: Claim for a grade (Pass or Fail)

Fifth-Grade Project 2013: RubeGoldBridge Problem
School: The Hillbrook School (Los Gatos, California)
Curriculum Designer: Christa Flores

At Hillbrook School, students receive grades, even for electives. In an effort to protect a growth mindset around process and creativity, grades are based not on working prototypes or tests or rubrics but on a pass/fail point system. Giving points for the written or visual submission of an argument works here because the only way to lose points is to turn in work late. Self-assessments such as these can be used effectively when the criteria for quality is cocreated with the students. Students also feel more comfortable grading themselves when the defense of pass or fail is concrete. Students are asked to show evidence of their own learning, either soft skills or measurable skills.

When students are asked to list reasons why they earned their grade, they are encouraged to list all the things that represented new learning or growth in an area they had been working in. Using this system, a teacher can support the wide range of learning that is happening in a self-directed learning space. Students will self-report using above-grade-level math skills to solve problems, using specialized tools for measurement, practicing new leadership skills, learning a new technology like programming or CAD, and so on. The claim/evidence/reasoning or persuasive essay format (which can be a movie made in Explain Everything[1] for students who struggle with writing) is only one form of assessment that encourages students to defend and reflect on their learning. A public showcase of work[2] also allows students to communicate their understanding of their problem to an audience.

An example of how this can be done with fifth graders can be seen at the end of the four-month-long "spring hard problem." The project is based on a prompt of three to five rules such as the following: (1) Do work on a 75-gram steel ball (move the ball from position A to B), (2) with an input and output that connects to two other teams' machines, (3) and bridges two or more forms of energy. After months of trial and error, design and redesign, and team building, it was clear that the students were having a very rich experience, but accessing it and getting it out in the open or even on paper was a huge challenge. This provided an opportunity to implement self-assessment.

Dear 5th Grade,

I am so proud of all of you. You survived PbS 5 iteration #1 and Maker Faire 2013! I know that I had some fails this year and I know I had some successes. Thank you for all of your hard work this year, especially the last four months during the Rube Gold Bridge problem. As many of you might feel that more time would have been better, I hope that you still found deep satisfaction with what you did accomplish.

While I am very sad to leave you at this important time, I am also looking forward to spending a week with the 6th grade in Yosemite this week to rest from Maker Faire and Maker Faire rush week. While I am gone, I need you to do something for me. I won't have time to grade you on your work for the RGB problem. I need you to decide what grade you should receive for this project. Only you can do this now. Only you know how hard you worked and how much you learned. Please choose ONE from the following grades. You must give me three pieces of evidence to support this grade claim. You can ask for help from anyone if you need to get mentored doing this. You have one week from today to complete this task. Please bring your grade and all evidence to school to share with me on Tuesday after Memorial day.

PASS ———— PASS WITH HONORS

FAIL ———— FAIL WITH HONORS

Your Fan,

Christa

Figure 14.4: Letter requesting student self-assessment.

The letter in figure 14.4 is the first one I presented to these fifth graders. They had no problem explaining what they had done to support their team, the way they took risks, or problems they had solved. Their ability to make a valid argument was so impressive that I continue to use this form of assessment at the end of all projects, including electives. One student's self-assessment for the RubeGoldBridge problem is shown in figure 14.5.

This style of assessment allows students to use argument and communication skills that are appropriate for that student. It also shifts the role of assessing progress from the adult to the learner.

Notes

1. explaineverything.com
2. youtube.com/watch?v=cw6MzHGPRHM

May 20, 2013

The Rube Gold Bridge Problem
By: Olivia ▬▬▬▬

For the Rube Gold bridge Problem, I fall into the "Fail with Honors" category. My design failed in some places, but I put a ton of team effort into this and rarely ever was working on something else. At some times my teammates weren't the best of partners and occasionally left me to work on the design. Here are three pieces of evidence to support my claim;

*I worked really hard on a star structure that was later incorporated into our design. I nailed it into my structure so that it would be easier to transport. In this star, I used both mechanical and electrical energy. The spinning movement of the star uses mechanical energy. The NXT robot the star ran on used electrical energy.

*I came up with the idea of making the ball go down tubes while an underwater movie was playing. Although we never had a movie play, we drew an underwater scene on the backdrop. Later on, we changed the backdrop completely and I helped make it, design it, and put the tube on. At MakerFaire, the tube came off and I taped it on.

Figure 14.5: Student self-assessment.

Making It Happen: Society + Inclusion

Making in education is not about having the coolest, most expensive tools or the fanciest makerspace. Making is a way to empower people to solve their own problems and develop the skills and mindsets to do so.

At its core, the maker movement is about sharing ideas and access to solutions with the world, not for money or power, but to make the world a better place. It's about trusting other people—often people you don't know—to use these ideas for good.

Making in the classroom is also about power and trust, and perhaps in an even more important way, because it's about transferring power to the learner—young people who are the ones who will take over the world in the not-too-distant future. And in giving learners agency and responsibility over their own learning, they gain trust—not just the trust of the adults in the room, but trust in themselves as powerful problem solvers and agents of change.

Making is not only a stance toward taking back that power, as individuals and communities, but also trusting ourselves and each other to share that power to create, learn, grow, and solve problems. Empowering youth is an act of showing trust by transferring power and agency to the learner. Helping young people learn how to handle the responsibility that goes along with this power is the sensible way to do it. Creating opportunities to develop student voice and agency takes skill and determination. Inspiring them with modern tools and knowledge needed to solve real problems is part of this job.

15

STEAM, the Trojan Horse for Making "Inclusivity"

by Christa Flores and Patrick Benfield

Many years ago when Christa was looking at undergraduate programs in anthropology and paleontology, a UC Berkeley graduate student (who happened to be a white male) snickered at the suggestion that it would be "fun" to work on a campus with so many fields of science to learn from. "It's way too competitive for collaboration," he scoffed, half disgusted, half proud to be surviving in such an environment. However, as a budding anthropologist, Christa knew that the ability to collaborate and form alliances to solve problems was a key survival strategy for early humans. Female humans, especially, have enjoyed evolutionarily success solving hard problems in this manner (Fukuyama 1998), so that grad student's description of how science was done really struck the wrong chord.

In more recent years, concern has mounted about attracting females and minorities to STEM fields. Counterbalancing past bias (by creating "unfair" advantages) to bridge the gap in college and STEM fields continues to be a messy road, however. Women still face constant doubts about whether they belong in the programs at top STEM schools. Competitive language from peers such as "[MIT is] turning away qualified applicants in favor of less-qualified female applicants" creates an environment of doubt (Selvage 2014) and does little to attract those to STEM already feeling less armed to compete.

Toy companies riding the wave of interest to close the gender gap in STEM have seen some success in sales, but simply adding storylines and product lines that feature girls in female-associated settings feels bereft of the kind of substantive changed needed. Getting more women to participate in the creation, versus consumption, of their lives through STEM careers is a conversation that can be easily lost in arguments for economic success. Take "The Case for Gender Equality" statement put out by the World Economic Forum for *The Global Gender Gap Index 2014*, which says: "The 'consumer case', 'talent case' and the 'diversity case' are all reflected in the findings around a growing business case for gender diversity. As women become more economically independent, they also become more significant consumers of goods and services, including for the majority of purchasing decisions of the household."

Sylvia Martinez links the importance, as well as challenge, of using self-directed learning[1] environments to support more outsiders such as girls in engineering (2014). She also points out that girls, on average, will interact with self-direction differently than boys. This looks like girls tending toward pleasing the teacher (or from my experience their friends or teammates) and avoiding conflict over scarce resources (that includes the teacher's attention). "Teachers need to remember that their suggestions carry a great amount of weight. To counter this and encourage self-directed learning, teachers need to train themselves to offer neutral, yet encouraging support for students to think outside the box," says Martinez. Furthermore, girls need to be given strategically "unfair" advantages by being invited by the adult to learn technology first, leading to leadership roles in the classroom as mentors.

More hope for closing the gap between STEM interest and underserved populations can be seen in the work of the nonprofit Maker Education Initiative in schools.[2] Due to its extensive work with public schools, the target audience for its initiatives is often low-income or minority students. In a news article targeting Latino families describing the role of creativity and how traditional schools fail to teach or preserve it (Bouza 2014), maker education was mentioned as a potential cure. In the article, Nirvan Mullick, a US documentary filmmaker and founder of the Imagination Foundation, says the emergence of these new educational initiatives "shows we're going through a period of transition, of changes in which we're experimenting and reimagining the way in which young people learn."

Similar efforts to combine issues of gender and income can be seen by the fact that over 50 percent of graduating engineering students at Harvey Mudd College are female. Why? President Maria Klawe, the first female president of Harvey Mudd, says it's easier than might be imagined. Female students are thriving in newly designed environments for collaboration and creative team projects. Avoiding lecturing helps too, notes Klawe. That way you avoid only two or three students dominating the dialog. Most importantly Klawe adds, "What we see happen when we [change teaching styles] is that it not only increases the number of women in those classes, it also increases the number of students of color and others who don't often feel like the dominant group in engineering or computer science" (Issacson 2014). Good learning environments support more students, period.

Figure 15.2: We like white coats, too, in a gender-neutral (outside) classroom.

If STEM is experiencing a new pushback for its competitive nature, as well as a peeling back of the layers of authority coded by the "white coat,"[3] then what does STEAM (insert *maker education* if you will) offer this conversation about change (Erickson and Kneller 2002)?

If STEM is still tied to marketability and the arts are stereotypically not marketable, then what can be the result of such a hybrid between the arts and STEM and making?

As far as inclusivity, when it comes to using STEAM as an argument for making in schools, we get to decide and define for ourselves exactly what *A* means. We can tailor it to match the skills, interests, and passions of our students (fig. 15.1). It can include cultural heritage—their native language, customs, or gender identity (fig 15.2). It also increases the umbrella of interested students who, for a variety of reasons (low self-esteem, fear of looking smart and/or nerdy, and so forth), might be willing to participate in making activities because they can express themselves in a way that connects with them. The *A* in *STEAM* is the wild card that gives a voice to our students in ways that a metric-driven focus on STEM cannot. That voice can and should be the seed of inclusivity at schools.

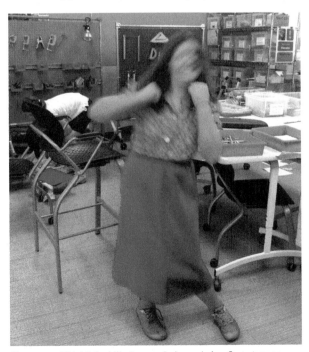

Figure 15.1: This high-skilled young lady made her first vintage redesign in the iLab's textiles section.

Notes

1. nais.org/Magazines-Newsletters /ISMagazine/Pages/Self Directed -Learning.aspx
2. makered.org/maker-caucus-brings-attention -to-the-need-for-more-diversity-in-making/
3. radiolab.org/story/91545-the-white-coat/

References

Blikstein, P. (2014, October 24). "I have guts too." Opening keynote address presented at FabLearn 2014, Stanford University. Retrieved from edstream.stanford.edu/Video/Play /5e5ea4447c2c4af597c03f3241054fea1d

Bouza, T. (2014, November 26). Initiatives seek to tap into children's creativity. Fox News Latino. Retrieved from latino.foxnews.com/latino /news/2014/11/26/initiatives-seek-to-tap -into-children-creativity/

Erickson, F., & Kneller, G. F. (2002, November). Comment: Culture, rigor, and science in educational research. *Educational Researcher, 31*(8), 21–24. Retrieved from edr.sagepub.com /content/31/8/21.short

Fukuyama, F. (1998, September–October). Women and the evolution of world politics. *Foreign Affairs, 77*(5).

Issacson, B. (2014, July). Why most of this college's engineering students are women. *Huffington Post.* Retrieved from huffingtonpost.com/2014/07/31/women-in -engineering_n_5631834.html

Martinez, S. (2014, November 3). What a girl wants: Self-directed learning, technology, and gender [Blog post]. Retrieved from sylviamartinez.com/what-a-girl-wants-self -directed-learning-technology-and-gender/

Selvage, J. (2014, November). Pushing women and people of color out of science before we go in. [Blog post]. *Huffington Post.* huffingtonpost.com/jennifer-selvidge /pushing-women-and-people-_b_5840392.html

World Economic Forum. (2014). The case for gender equality. *The Global Gender Gap Index 2014.* World Economic Forum. Retrieved from reports.weforum.org/global-gender -gap-report-2014/part-1/the-case-for-gender -equality/

The Young Papaneks: In the Face of a Problem, a Project

by Gilson Domingues and Pietro Domingues

Brazilians live in a country with a lot of problems and as a result have developed many ways to solve them, not all of them "orthodox." Of course, having flexible rules can lead to ethical problems, which must be corrected. But the good side of this adaptative characteristic of Brazilian people is that we are natural-born designers. The important thing is to see the real problems and solve them in a way that benefits the entire (global) community.

Our work is inspired by architect and designer Victor Papanek, a designer and educator who believed in inclusive and responsible design. In 1960, he was already working on what today we call sustainable design. His work permeates our activities not only conceptually but also in the modus operandi, giving importance to low-cost materials and simpler solutions (fig. 16.1).

Figure 16.1: Tin-can radio design by Victor Papanek.

The advantage in using this kind of material isn't just about cost and access. By designing a system to avoid trash accumulation (fig. 16.2) we not only make our urban environment better, we also find new renewable resources. When reusing the resources, students learn about reverse engineering and how to adapt any material we have on hand to meet our objectives.

Figure 16.2: Solution for collecting garbage created by our students.

Designers at all ages

It's clear that for each age range there is a different mode of reading the world, and because of this, a child has a different agenda than an adult or a teenager.

Child designers

Design is always centered on human beings and what they do. For children, this is often play. Because of this, at the Alef School in Rio de Janeiro we created a course called Arte, Tecnologia e Design (Arts, Technology, and Design), where we worked with toys and fabrication in two situations:

- Eighth graders made their own GoGo Mini (a low-cost robotics board), and in groups they built a robot using the board. They learned how to program, and at the end they used the robot as a basis for a big kinetic and interactive toy (fig. 16.3).
- Sixth graders made a simple kinetic toy, using things like cardboard boxes and other discarded materials plus motors and in some cases the GogoBoard. They also created curious interactive experiences, for example, a mirror that answers whether the user is beautiful (fig. 16.4).[1]

This experience of making a toy is really very motivating. In Colégio Santo Américo, a private school in São Paulo, the students created their own oscillator toys and then modified them.

Figure 16.3: Eighth-grade kinetic toy designs.

Figure 16.4: Sixth-grade kinetic toy designs.

The toys move on their own due to the motor oscillations (fig. 16.5). Using a variation of this oscillator, children can build a piano using multiple buttons.[2]

Figure 16.5: Kinetic toy testing.

High schoolers: The young Newtons reading the world with scientific experiments

Unfortunately in Brazil scientific education is very deficient, especially in public schools. In 2003 Colégio Santo Américo created a digital inclusion project aimed at needy communities in the region. The project gained strength with the support of Dr. Blikstein in 2004. In 2007 he implemented an introductory scientific program. Spontaneously, the students started to research

subjects of their own interest (e.g., global warming, earthquakes, volcanoes), and they made scale models to validate their knowledge obtained from books and the Internet (fig. 16.6).

Figure 16.6: Students learn that building things can help them understand scientific principles to build things even better.

Naturally the models not only helped them understand abstract concepts, the models helped them articulate these concepts in a creative way. In addition they felt excited to solve both technical and scientific problems.

Teenagers

While younger children see the world with imagination and in a ludic way, teenagers use their creativity associated with their incipient critical vision of the world. In Colégio Santo Américo we had the opportunity to work with students to find solutions that would be important to the world. For example, students designed a telepresence system in which the operator uses a manipulator that moves the arm over long distances (fig. 16.7).

Figure 16.7: Student-designed telepresence systems.

We always try to encourage the creation of new ideas (figs. 16.8 and 16.9). Every idea is good; it just needs to fit in its place and moment. Then we create a "bank of ideas," where students can store their ideas and share them or use them later.

Figure 16.8: Air-cooled clothes.

Figure 16.11: Students being interviewed by media about their inventions.

The best thing about these fairs is the opportunity for these students to interact and share with other people who develop the same kind of projects and talk about their ideas as philosophers from ancient Greece did in Agoras (figs. 16.11–16.13).

Figure 16.9: Wind-powered car.

Figure 16.12: Meeting people from around the world who share a passion for design and invention.

The young Platos, Socrateses, Aristotles, and other philosophers on the Agora of science fairs

Participating in design praxis, the application of design to real life, is captivating and offers great experiences. Many of the students who experienced this process solved problems and developed social projects even without explicitly knowing it. All of the projects showed the following elements, which are important criteria for science fairs in Brazil:

- Social relevance
- Economic viability
- Technical and scientific tradition-based projects
- Generation of innovation

These projects participated in these science fairs, and one was even selected to participate in INTEL-ISEF in 2006. This project was a public telephone that adjusts itself automatically to the user's height, whether a child or wheelchair user (fig. 16.10).[3] It achieved tremendous success both in Brazil and the United States.

Figure 16.13: Positive media coverage of young people.

Creating designers—undergraduate design course

The maker culture is not limited to the school. There are professional activities that have the maker culture as its kernel. Using the prototyping process creates better projects and better designers. This is how the maker culture contributes to design, architecture, and engineering.

At Universidade Anhembi Morumbi, in São Paolo, I have been working on many aspects of the maker culture. One part is related to prototyping and digital fabrication in an undergraduate digital design and architecture course that uses 3D printers and laser cutters. The other part is related to game design, where the students also learn how to prototype electronic circuits

Figure 16.10: Ergorelhao: adjustable-height public telephone design.

and microcontroller-based devices while making games:

- Students made virtual reality games using the Occulus Rift headset (fig. 16.14).
- Students created Arduino-based interfaces to allow a joystick to communicate with the Unity game engine.[4]
- Students built their own sensors to save money and understand how the electronics work.[5]
- Students built robots controlled by cell phone via Bluetooth.[6]

Figure 16.14: Sailing simulator prototype with Occulus Rift.

Makers forever

As we have seen, being a maker is not limited to an age range. Many professionals are continuously learning about what is new in the market and because of that, a lot of people are starting to embrace the maker movement.

When we ran a 3D printing assembly course that was open to the public, the participants were adults of all ages. People of many different professions were very interested in the potential of this new technology and culture of the maker movement (fig. 16.15). That just shows that being a maker has no limits!

Figure 16.15: Building prototypes.

Notes

1. youtube.com/watch?v=1_d3gMAKt2g&feature= youtu.be
2. fablearn.stanford.edu/fellows/project/piano
3. csasp.g12.br/conteudo/oColegio/projetos /responsabilidadeSocial/tecnologia/robotica /projetos/ergoOrelhao/Default.aspx
4. Tutorial on using Arduino as a joystick to communicate to Unity, a game engine (in Portuguese): guiaarduino.wordpress.com /2015/04/09/joysticks-especiais-integrando -jogos-eletronicos-e-arduino /Also youtu.be/fOLRmziBTEU
5. Tutorial on how to make a sensor: fablearn.stanford.edu/fellows/project /force-resisting-diy
6. fablearn.stanford.edu/fellows/project /bluetooth-robot

"Making" in California K–12 Education: A Brief State of Affairs

by David Malpica

In schools, what is now called maker education was been known for many years as hands-on project-based learning (PBL). While maker education continues to deepen its roots in small pockets of the nation's private education, the introduction and implementation of making into California public education still has a long road to go.

Some of these efforts can be seen in the bubbling California charter school movement, with the most well-known and established programs running in the High Tech High network of San Diego, the LightHouse Community Charter School of Oakland, and a few other public schools spread throughout the state. In district-managed schools, Fab Lab Richmond was the first full-blown digital fabrication space to serve a large public school community: the entire preK–12 population of West Contra Costa Unified School District. Also funded by Chevron and designed in cooperation with the Fab Foundation, another Fab Lab is planned for Bakersfield. Castlemont High School in Oakland has opened a Fab Lab this year. Ravenswood City School District in East Palo Alto has an ambitious plan to set up seven makerspaces. This shows the clustered efforts in a handful of school districts out of the thousand-plus in California. The construction or setup of dedicated project-based learning spaces is by no means a perfect metric for this daunting task as many other programs exist without them. However, at the current rate, and with a growing K–12 population of over 6.5 million students, Maker Education Initiative's (MakerEd's) inspirational motif "Every child a maker" will take an indefinite amount of time to achieve in California.

MakerEd, a nonprofit headquartered in Oakland, is the biggest player in efforts to support maker education in and out of state. MakerEd has released information claiming to impact more than "140,000 youth and families" through a diverse set of "youth-serving organizations" across twenty-four states (Maker Ed 2014). When asked about its impact in the California public school arena, Steve Davee, director of education at MakerEd, said: "The best number based on events, our PD, and MakerEd direct relationships is at least sixty-four public schools, with easily hundreds more schools benefiting in other ways. . . ."[1] It is clear there is growing interest in the adoption of maker education practices by teachers in many schools in California.

Teacher preparation and pedagogy

Meanwhile, it seems that California is behind in offering credentialed teacher preparation dealing with innovative hands-on subject matter and curricula. It is unclear how many graduates out of California undergraduate STEM and graduate education programs head into the field of project-based teaching and learning as opposed to educational app entrepreneurship, MOOCS, or even traditional textbook classrooms. Another concern has to do with the focus on STEM, which alone may be too narrow to solve the challenges of engaging diverse populations in the state. The first experience of making most children are exposed to is art; why is it being left out later in life? Some of the most astounding contemporary art is enabled by STE(A)M. Furthermore, curriculum designed largely by a homogenous population cannot truly serve a heterogenous one.

Advocates of PBL have stated that while introducing any kind of making into education is a positive move forward, it would be better served being accompanied by a shift in pedagogy. The typical practices of textbook and worksheet instruction, student grading, and testing are known to contribute to the development of fixed mindsets, the opposite desired outcome of maker education in youth. A welcome development in teacher training is being spearheaded at Sonoma State University with its Maker Certificate Program. With a clear and sound set of educational values, it stands apart from the sea of typical math and science education and teacher preparation designed to be instructed, graded, and tested.

Another pedagogical challenge is that of finding the right balances. Any kind of truly deep project-based learning takes significant time and multidisciplinary facilitation. This means teachers of different subject areas need to collaborate on unit integration. A true innovation in education would be to acknowledge the need for time and expertise brought in by teachers with a growth mindset, which goes beyond the standard fragmented curriculum of math, science, and English language arts (ELA). Making in the classroom will not get the time and attention it deserves while math and ELA still occupy most of the curriculum time. This is unfortunately still an effect left behind, almost ironically, by No Child Left Behind practices, which emphasized math and English.

Standards and assessment

Another push that opens up making opportunities in the California public school system has to do with the newly adopted Next Generation Science Standards. While pedagogically standards are a divisive issue, the Next Generation Science Standards actually do a good job of adding engineering practices into the mix of science while leaving the field very open for content development. Currently, there appear to be no plans to add specific engineering content into the California Standards Tests (and these won't be dramatically changed in four or five years). We can only be proactive in addressing California education leadership to see the benefits of keeping it grade- and test-free, allowing opportunities for different kinds of making and engineering to be taught and in order to meet and make use of local needs and expertise. A very worthwhile effort of developing alternative assessment in the shape of open portfolios is being conducted by MakerEd in partnership with Indiana University. FabLearn Fellow Christa Flores has compiled and constructed important recommendations in this area. Another alternative method of assessment comes from

Stanford University: choice-based assessment. When confronted with problems, do students persevere or find creative solutions instead of giving up? A new framework of assessment is important, as research on career paths has shown interest is a more powerful and enduring driving force than concrete skill-set building.

Conclusion and suggested next steps

Only through a concerted effort of state and federal government, nonprofits, institutions and industry, redesigned pedagogy and assessment methods, teacher collaboration, curriculum integration, and compromise will it be possible to reach the California student population in the short amount of time needed to build a homebrewed generation of empowered and innovative makers, engineers, artists, and designers. With the current momentum and excitement around maker education, and with the state of California carefully recovering from years of deficit, there are now opportunities to regain funding. Said funding would be well used to propose and execute student-centered programs designed to build agency, interest, and growth mindsets. Colleges and universities would do schools and families a big favor by accepting portfolios (perhaps in place of grades and test scores) and looking for students demonstrating strong interests and good choice making. If this was a statewide (and why not nationwide?) policy, schools and government policy makers would adapt and teach what matters instead of what is easy to grade and test. Ultimately, it is the stakeholders who would benefit the most from becoming active in recognizing and demanding an education centered around what matters most.

Note

1. S. Davee, personal communication, February 2, 2015

Reference

Maker Ed. (2014, June 25). Maker Ed announces incredible progress on Maker Corps Program at CGI America. Maker Education Initiative. Retrieved from makered.org/maker-ed -announces-incredible-progress-on -maker-corps-program-at-cgi-america/

18 Making for Change

by Roy Ombatti

In the Nairobi Fab Lab, at the University of Nairobi in Kenya, I have personally seen that hands-on making is life changing. However it can be difficult to measure impact, and as such it is difficult to quantify the successes of the process. But I am particularly curious about making in the context of the developing world. I feel the impact of the change effected by making is most significantly felt—and needed—here. But then how do we ensure that making is exploited to its full potential?

With developing world challenges such as reliable connectivity and off-the-grid access to electricity, there is a tremendous need for ingenuity and innovation. The issue is how to provide making experiences to those brilliant young minds. From my travels around East Africa, I am amazed at the number of small creative and innovative spaces. Africans have clearly seen the need for local solutions to local problems. The making scene has become really vibrant in the last few years. The potential and need for African makers is tremendous, and makerspaces are popping up, including in schools.

I was very impressed by the Accelerating Innovation and Social Entrepreneurship (AISE) space in Arusha, Tanzania. AISE is a local innovation space where the community is empowered to design and create its own solutions and technologies. It is a space where creative ideas come to life. I spent two months working with AISE earlier this year. Its scope recently expanded to hosting workshops for schoolchildren, teaching them skills required for making as well as getting them involved in project-based learning.

The focus on children is so important to improve education and lives around the world but especially in the developing world. There is a need for similar spaces all over Africa in order to ensure the systemic and sustainable development of Africa.

19

3D Printing in Kenya

by Roy Ombatti

In 2012, 3D printing in Kenya became a reality when the Nairobi Fab Lab received the first 3D printer in Kenya. In three short years, the trend had caught on to the point of individual Kenyans owning personal printers.

In early December 2014 I presented at a conference on Footwear Health Tech in Eindhoven, Netherlands, about the Happy Feet project, which was providing footwear to people with foot deformities. During the conference, 3D printing featured prominently as there is clear value in the custom fit and personalization of shoes. I mentioned that, as a result of my research, I had concluded that it wasn't yet time for "meaningful" and sustainable 3D printing in Kenya, especially for what I was trying to do and on such a large scale. I was asked why this was so because 3D printing (printers and filament) had become very inexpensive. I explained that the affordability of the printers was relative, and the Kenyan context is a different one altogether. Further persistent questioning about 3D printer affordability got me thinking how to make 3D printing affordable in an African context.

This is something I had been trying to do for a while because for a long time this project relied heavily on 3D printing. I had thought of how to recycle certain plastic waste materials to extrude plastic filament. From my travels, I had seen that there was already a lot going on in this field. And I am happy to say that I set up our own extruder in Nairobi in early 2015.

And then there's brilliant African ingenuity such as thirty-three-year-old inventor Kodjo Afate Gnikou in Togo, West Africa. Stories such as his building a functioning 3D printer mostly from e-waste[1] gave me renewed hope in the maker culture in Africa. Unique situations call for unique solutions. Our circumstances give us new ways of thinking, and I am looking forward to what this amazing continent has to offer.

So why not do the same in Kenya? Challenge accepted! I have made significant strides toward realizing this goal with African Born 3D Printing (AB3D).[2] AB3D is a social enterprise involved with the production of local and affordable 3D printers as well as 3D printing filament from waste materials. The 3D printers are made from electronic waste parts while the filament is extruded from recycled PET plastic waste. The progress of our printer design is shown in figure 19.1. The goal of AB3D is to alleviate poverty, make 3D printing more reachable and affordable to makers in Kenya, and hopefully make high-quality products that could be sold to the international market. Part of this agenda is to establish makerspaces in schools centered around, although not limited to, 3D printing.

Figure 19.1: AB3D's Retr3D_V2 printer (left) alongside Retr3D_V1 (right).

Notes

1. treehugger.com/gadgets/african-inventor-makes-3d-printer-e-waste-video.html
2. africanborn3dprinting.strikingly.com

Technologies of the Heart: Beyond #BlackLivesMatter and toward #MakingLiberation

by Susan Klimczak, in collaboration with Adia Wallace and Nettrice Gaskins

One 2015 collaborative project at the South End Technology Center @ Tent City (SETC) in Boston, Massachusetts, was supported by the Harvard Graduate School of Education (HGSE) Dean's Equity Project. The goal was to create a safe and creative space for high school and college youth to explore their identities and their relationship to issues that have come up in the #BlackLivesMatter movement through activities based on hip-hop culture. Then, using the design engineering process, the youth imagined a world that would work for everyone by creating participatory art and technology projects and activities that engaged them in #MakingLiberation. These were shared during demonstrations and workshops for the HGSE community and served as inspiration for other youth during the 2015 Learn 2 Teach, Teach 2 Learn (L2TT2L) program.

> *If we want a society and culture that works for everyone, we need innovation in our relationships along with innovation in the STEM fields and STEM education.*
>
> —Mel King, activist and founder of South End Technology Center @Tent City

In our thirteen-year-old STEAM maker program at L2TT2L, we most often start designing teaching activities by identifying the big ideas and skills connected to the technology we teach, whether computer and physical programming, electronics, digital design, or fabrication. We call these "technologies of the Earth." Then we work to create a "cool," culturally relevant activity that engages the youth in those big ideas and skills.

What excited me about this project is that we were *decentering*, or taking these technologies of the Earth away from the focus of activity design and putting them in the service of "technologies of the heart"—technologies that are necessary to bring out the best in us and enhance our relationships with each other.

What has most engaged me as an educator for the past few years is a participatory research project with youth teachers and college mentors that seeks to document how the technologies of the heart support the STEAM education of our Boston youth of color. I've shared my thoughts about this in some of my FabLearn Fellow blog posts.[1]

At SETC during the school year, we have two small after-school programs for teenagers:

Eek! Electronics Explorers Klub, and Fab Stewards program. During circle-up sessions, the teen participants expressed how they were discouraged (and even banned) from talking about #BlackLivesMatter at school or participating in the nationwide school walkout. Some spoke about how their parents were afraid to talk about #BlackLivesMatter and asked them not to participate in any activities. Their lack of meaningful opportunities at school or at home to explore and express their ideas and feelings about the #BlackLivesMatter movement concerned me because the courage and ideas of youth have historically been at the center of social movements here and across the planet.

I am also beginning to understand #BlackLivesMatter as a maker movement that indeed is seeking to create new technologies of the heart (and Earth!) to address social justice issues. So, in collaboration with graduate student Adia Wallace from the Technology and Innovation in Education program at the Harvard Graduate School of Education, we developed a successful proposal to the HGSE Dean Equity Fellowship to address this question: "How can science, technology, engineering, and math enrichment help youth of color meaningfully express their feelings and address issues related to #BlackLivesMatter in historically and culturally relevant ways in Boston, Massachusetts?"

Strategies for engaging the community

"Our ultimate end must be the creation of the beloved community." —Martin Luther King Jr.

Engaging people from the local community in maker education projects enriches education for our youth and brings fresh vitality into the programming. Visiting educators can serve as role models and expose youth to possible STEM career paths. Many talented people are also seeking ways to give back to their communities and have creative outlets for their talents beyond work. The question often is "How do educators go about 'making' these relationships?"

At SETC's L2TT2L program, we used a number of practical strategies in developing collaborative partners for "Beyond #BlackLivesMatter & Towards #MakingLiberation: Using Hip Hop & STEAM to Provide Opportunities for Youth to Explore and Express Possibilities for Change."

Strategy 1: Seek role models who look like our youth

As a white education organizer working for over a decade with 90 percent youth of color in our L2TT2L, I know I bring much love and skill to our youth. However, I feel it is particularly important for them to experience role models who not only look like them but have developed effective and interesting STEM skills and exemplary achievements in the community as well as in higher education. So, I work hard to find those community members who look like our youth and can share their talents and stories through social media and networking (fig. 20.1).

Strategy 2: Cultivate long-term relationships with local programs and individuals in higher-education institutions

Over the past twelve years, L2TT2L has developed a lively and deep relationship with the MIT Media Lab, including the Lifelong Kindergarten Group (LLK) and the High-Low Technology Group. Our youth have been among the early testers and adopters of LLK technology education tools such

Figure 20.1: 2014 youth teachers with LLK graduate student Abdulrahman Idbli in Chain Reaction Workshop at MIT Media Lab.

as Scratch, PICO Crickets, MaKey MaKeys, and Chibitronics Circuit Stickers.

Strategy 3: Involve youth, as they are the best ambassadors for developing community relationships

When LLK researcher Dr. Karen Brennan moved to the faculty at the Harvard Graduate School of Education, she asked Dr. Amon Millner and me to serve as guest speakers about our work with L2TT2L in her T-550 course called Designing for Learning by Making.

Amon and I decided that we could have the most impact on the Designing for Learning by Making graduate students at Harvard by bringing youth teachers as guest speakers and having them showcase some of their projects. The adults provided some history and a few contextual comments here and there but made sure that the youth teachers were lifted up as the main speakers. Technologies of the heart can involve giving youth opportunities to experience and communicate what is significant to them about learning by making.

We recruited third-year youth teacher Naeem Wilson and first-year youth teacher Cynthia Johnson to speak to the class (fig. 20.2). I contacted the headmaster and principal at their high schools, as well as their parents, to explain how this opportunity could enrich the education of the youth *and* the Harvard graduate students. This allowed us to get written permission for them to miss school one morning. We also packed up some of the youth projects to showcase at their

Figure 20.3: Adia Wallace with youth teacher Tyla in a playful moment during Eek! Electronics Explorers Klub.

Figure 20.2: Dr. Karen Brennan with L2TT2L youth teachers Cynthia Johnson and Naeem Wilson at Harvard Graduate School of Education.

Harvard talk.

Naeem and Cynthia were "rock stars" at the class, and our guest speaking time was extended well beyond what had been planned in order to accommodate the many questions from the Harvard graduate students. It turned out that Cynthia and Naeem were not just the only youth to speak to the class—they were among the very few guest speakers of color. Their impact was palpable, especially on the graduate students of color.

Strategy 4: Mentor local education students and community members

As a result of this Harvard visit, I received many e-mails from graduate students. One student, Adia Wallace from Mississippi, visited our technology center and began hanging out with our youth in her "spare" time (fig. 20.3). She even participated in our Digital Embroidery and Sewing Group and helped out with our youth teachers' holiday pop-up store. Her infectious enthusiasm made developing relationships with the youth come quickly and easily.

Strategy 5: Participate in local STEM professional networks

Practicing technologies of the heart involves creating caring community connections that support the maker activities of youth. Adia wanted to have local STEAM educators participate in our collaborative Beyond #BlackLivesMatter and Toward

#MakingLiberation project. I began to introduce her to people in our local Race, Education, and Democracy STEM network, which seeks to provide meaningful STEM opportunities for educators and youth of color. This network grew out of the wonderful Simmons College Race, Education, and Democracy Lecture and Book series directed by Professor Theresa Perry.

In the fall of 2014 the RED STEM Network held an event that featured a makerspace panel for local educators and parents at the SETC. One of the most engaging speakers was the new STEAM lab director of the Boston Arts Academy, Dr. Nettrice

Figure 20.4: Dr. Nettrice Gaskins, STEAM lab director of the Boston Arts Academy, speaking at the event.

Gaskins (fig. 20.4).[2]

Adia, Nettrice, and I met together several times for lively conversations, imagining how hip-hop culture and Afrofuturism could be incorporated into the project. Nettrice generously offered to participate as a collaborator. Her unique approach to maker education helped both Adia and me expand our own understanding and practice of culturally responsive making, breathing a new vitality into our work.

Strategy 6: Use design thinking for planning with hip-hop culture as a framework

To plan, Adia and I gathered interested people from our support network over an after-work take-out dinner to imagine what we could do with youth in the #MakingLiberation activity. Using ideation techniques from design thinking, we asked them to write all their ideas on sticky notes. Then we arranged the sticky notes into categories on a whiteboard until an activity plan emerged (fig. 20.5).

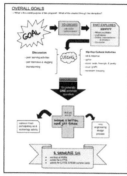

Figure 20.5: Organizing the ideas imagined on sticky notes into a map to create a clear goal for the activities.

This led us to define what the youth would do:

- Use hip-hop expressions such as cyphers, graffiti (fig. 20.6), and spoken word to engage in authentic conversations regarding identity and bigotry
- Be exposed to hip-hop maker culture and its techno-innovations
- Build knowledge together through constructionism, a theory of learning through making developed by Seymour Papert
- Use technology as both the medium and the message

Figure 20.6: Graffiti created by youth participants.

Strategy 7: Spend significant time exploring the issue and what is important to the youth

One important decision we made was to spend about half of the sessions exploring #BlackLivesMatter before beginning project design and building. Nettrice Gaskins led discussion "cyphers" about the often-overlooked maker geniuses of hip-hop. Technologies of the heart can involve helping youth to develop relationships between a culture in which they participate and its history of making and electronic innovation. Nettrice explains:[3]

> Hip-hop artists Grandmaster Flash and Afrika Bambaataa, along with a few others, pioneered what we now know to be hip-hop music and culture. Grandmaster Flash is credited with the invention of the first cross-fader or audio mixer by reclaiming parts from a junkyard in the Bronx. Flash also advanced the technique of scratching, which is a DJ and turntablist technique used to produce distinctive sounds. Scratch programming was inspired by this method of music production.

> Africa Bambaataa created "turntablism" as its own sub-genre and helped to make electronic music a popular trend in the late 1990s. He picked up on sci-fi imagery and cosmic ideas from the 1960s and 1970s including the style of jazz maverick Sun Ra, who is known as the grandfather of Afrofuturism, which is a style of storytelling that treats African American themes and addresses African American concerns in the context of 20th-century technoculture.

Nettrice helped youth explore hip-hop as a responsive and improvisational musical and sociopolitical movement for change. The youth participants also engaged in hands-on activities to explore the creative possibilities of expressing their thoughts and feelings through hip-hop culture including graffiti and poetry. We ended this imagining part of #MakingLiberation by having youth generate ideas for their own manifesto—ideas that would guide project building and appear on the #MakingLiberation workshop poster (fig. 20.7).

Figure 20.7: Poster for #MakingLiberation presentations at the Harvard Graduate School of Education that includes part of the manifesto that the youth generated.

Strategy 8: Use youth-generated engineering design-process steps to imagine, explore, design, and create projects

Technologies of the heart can involve helping youth to transform their relationships with maker education methods. A few years ago, I heard the youth teachers at L2TT2L having a conversation about the educational poster of the design engineering process that hung in our Fab Lab. They said, "This doesn't make any sense to us!" So we gathered a group of experienced youth teachers and college mentors and had them research and evaluate about a dozen engineering design

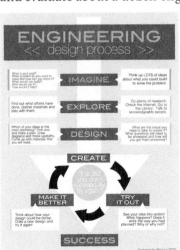

Figure 20.8: Design process infographic.

process diagrams that were used by groups as diverse as PBS Design Squad Nation and MIT graduate engineering classes. They decided that none of them really worked. So they generated their own. One of the

youth who was interested in graphic arts turned it into a simple and elegant infographic (fig. 20.8).

We have successfully used this infographic to guide our project-building activities for the past six years. Each year, in our evaluation survey, the youth have given us feedback that this version of the engineering design process works for them.

For #MakingLiberation, the youth generated project ideas and then formed small groups to rapidly prototype their ideas with materials we had on hand, have a design review to get feedback, then begin building their projects. The two projects that came out of this process were the United Voices Sequencer and the Rainbow Glove.

United Voices Sequencer

Tyla, Naeem, and Simon decided to use the idea of the sequencer, ubiquitously used in hip-hop music production, that uses words and sounds to convey a personal message about why the voices of all people matter. They designed and coded two Scratch programs for people to test (code for test program) and then play (final Scratch program) their messages using a MaKey MaKey controller (fig 20.9).

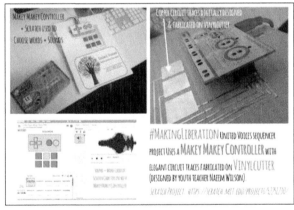

Figure 20.9: United Voices sequencer.

Rainbow Glove

Mariela, Antwain, and Steven were newbies to electronics and coding but were inspired by a project they saw at Adafruit called the "Piano-Glove"[4] that converts color to musical sounds. They decided to put their own spin on the glove by remixing it into a Rainbow Glove (fig. 20.10) that would demonstrate "It's OK for people to be different" and "Things are better with many colors and cultures of people." They also decided to use the "Let's Show Off" poem (see strategy 9) they

Figure 20.10: Mariela, Antwain, and Steven produced their own short video about the Rainbow Glove.

Figure 20.11: The poem "Let's Show Off" was discussed with activist and center director Mel King.

discussed with Mel King as a basis for this activity (fig. 20.11).

Technologies of the heart often involve helping youth articulate relationships between the ideas behind the technology they use and what they are up against in their own lives.

One of the most powerful parts of the Rainbow Glove project was the connection that Mariela made between the science of color and the impact of racism in her own life:

> To see color, you have to have light. When light shines on an object, some colors bounce off the object and others are absorbed by it. Our eyes only see the colors that are bounced off or reflected.

> Racism works that way too. People only see what's reflected back, not what is absorbed.

> In my own life, I absorb people's criticism of me. I absorb the negative feelings when they don't see who I really am and when they don't believe I am capable or smart.

Strategy 9: Create meaningful ways for youth to "show off," taking a page from constructionism by making projects truly "public entities"
Cultivating technologies of the heart means developing opportunities, especially for youth of color, to take what they create into the community to "show off" what they have accomplished. The poem "Let's Show Off" (fig. 20.12) says, "Let's diminish the misconceptions of [our youth] and the life that they lead." Making projects into what Seymour Papert called "public entities" also gives opportunities for youth to develop a belief in themselves—self-efficacy—and to learn more by explaining their projects and their process of designing, building, troubleshooting, and improving.

For #MakingLiberation, our Eek! Electronics Explorers presented their projects through demonstrations and a workshop for faculty and students at the Harvard Graduate School of Education and made a video.[5]

Figure 20.12: The poem "Let's Show Off."

Final Thoughts on #MakingLiberation

Adia Wallace offered some reflections on our #MakingLiberation experience:

> Susan and I witnessed struggle firsthand: the youth leaders struggling to understand where we were trying to go with our wrap-up lessons in history, sociology, and politics; the youth struggling to identify the problem first and imagine the solution second; the youth struggling with creative confidence. And the youth also witnessed our struggles: struggling to make sure that we can afford the technology kits with our budget; struggling to help them make connections—both in our wrap-up lessons and in teaching the new youth leaders how to solder small circuits; struggling to push them to realize their potential the same way we did.
>
> The best thing about presentation day was not only the technologies of the heart but also how seven uniquely amazing Boston youth could touch the hearts of fifteen attendees from the HGSE community through their love for technology. The youth captivated this audience by sharing their stories and by incorporating rhyme, culturally responsive techniques such as call-and-response and hip-hop (in addition to rap music influences), and demonstrating their diverse interests from graphic design to circuitry.
>
> There was much laughter in the room and tears of joy. Our workshops received several mentions and retweets on Twitter, and several peers either e-mailed me directly or told me in-person how much they'd thoroughly enjoyed the youth leaders. One of the HGSE staff members, a man of color, broke down after the workshops ended, expressing that L2TT2L is how his sons can flourish. The youth leaders were telling me even prior to the workshops that it was the best day they'd experienced that school year based on how excited the HGSE community was about the demo table. I could not agree more with the L2TT2L youth. Why? Because #YouthVoicesMatter."

Because #TechnologiesoftheHeartMatter. The center of my practice as a maker educator is reminding myself daily to not only focus on

Figure 20.13: Learn 2 Teach, Teach 2 Learn youth leaders.

engineering skills and ideas but to focus on those technologies that are necessary to bring out the best in us and enhance our relationships with each other (fig 20.13).

Notes

1. fablearn.stanford.edu/fellows/blog/some -thoughts-making-technologies-heart-while -thinking-seymour-papert
   Also fablearn.stanford.edu/fellows/blog /making-justice-youth-restoring -their-own-humanity-and-humanity-us-all
2. fablearn.stanford.edu/fellows/blog /dr-nettrice-gaskins-recontextualizing -makerspace-culturally-responsive-education
3. N. Gaskins, personal communication, March 2015
4. learn.adafruit.com/pianoglove
5. youtube.com/watch?v=7EVUy2oMrKI

Projects to Explore in Depth

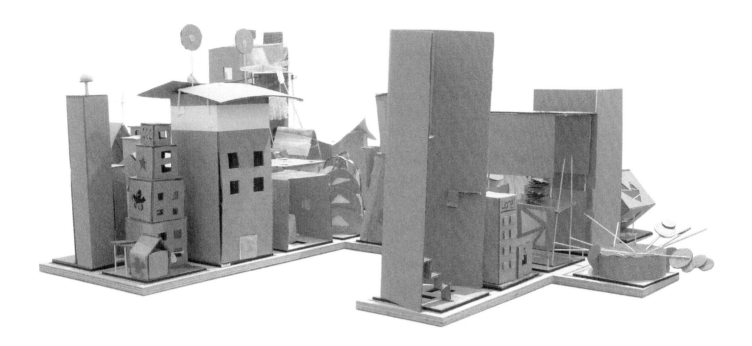

The projects in this section give the reader a lot to think about, try, and adapt for one's own situation. In contrast to the project snapshots in the final section of this book, these projects are more fully described and often feature interesting reflections and course corrections from the authors.

21 Of Feet, Fleas, and 3D Printing

by Roy Ombatti

I have been involved in many projects during my time at the FabLab in Nairobi, and I personally enjoy those that leverage technology for change and development. I am most interested in the space for technology in development because it is in this space that "making" is most needed. Hailing from a developing country, empowering people, primarily the poor, with the necessary knowledge and skills to make them problem solvers has never made more sense to me than it does now. Gone are the days of handouts and donor funds. That technique is clearly not working in the fight against poverty. The approach should be more practical as well as personal. The "poor" should be taught how to solve their own problems, supported through this process rather than being thrown money. This is where making comes in—whether high- or low-tech types of making. Amy Smith, founder of Massachusetts Institute of Technology's D-lab, which is building a global network of innovators to design and disseminate technologies that meaningfully improve the lives of people living in poverty said, "We need to think of poor people not as vulnerable but as capable. We have to think of it not as a billion mouths to feed but two billions hands to engage" (Bansal 2014).

A personal project of mine called Happy Feet involves leveraging 3D printing to fight jiggers that cause foot deformities and sometimes death. The jigger (fig. 21.1) is a small flea that is found in dirty environments. It feeds on the flesh and blood of its warm-blooded hosts. The female jigger buries itself in the host's flesh and lays eggs. This results in a black spot that is typically itchy and painful. Scratching ruptures the sac and spreads the infestation. There is stigma against the infection, and it affects millions of people, mostly chil-

Figure 21.1: A jigger.

dren. In Kenya alone there have been 265 reported deaths as a result of the jigger menace.

Besides poor hygiene, the common denominator among those affected by jiggers is abject poverty. They cannot afford water for cleaning as it is not a priority. This contributes greatly to the spread of the jigger menace. Many people cannot afford shoes, and the infected cannot fit into conventional shoes. The infected use needles to dig out the jiggers, but this is painful and contributes to the spread of diseases such as HIV/AIDS through the sharing of needles. Shoes are thus necessary in stopping the infection as the jiggers are poor at jumping.

One solution is 3D-printed, affordable, customized, and medicated shoes. This will involve setting up mobile shoe centers, tapping into the networks of Ahadi Kenya Trust (the only organization in Kenya tackling this issue), where people can come in and have their feet scanned and have part of the shoe printed for them.[1]

The magic of making is revealed in these shoe centers. These centers are not just about giving people shoes but spaces where the youth can be taught about basic shoe-making skills. Because 3D printing for the production of these shoes will be both expensive and very time-consuming, the printed parts of the shoe will be used as a frame around which a classical shoe can be constructed using locally available materials. In time, I'm sure these hurdles can be overcome. One goal is to teach the youth about 3D printing technology, encompassing basic CAD design principles as well basic computing and designing.

But why stop there? The solution to jiggers cannot be just shoes. The crux of the problem is poverty, and something needs to be done to directly address this. I hope to do this through maker education. With continued support, the shoe centers can serve as small-scale fab labs where the youth are taught skills and introduced to making. With these skills, the youth will certainly have a better chance at life as they not only feel like they are part of the solution but they are also empowered to do more—much, much more. This community space will serve as a second chance at life for them.

At press time, this is still at the proof-of-concept stage of the project. The teaching will at first be geared toward children (the most affected) and limited to basic computing and design. Ideally, the space will be a community-led initiative to ensure the sustainability of the project. If those in the community feel like they own the solution, then they will certainly protect it and ensure its success.

Note

1. 3dprint.com/25587/happy-feet-3d-printed -shoes/

Reference

Bansal, S. (2014, August 21). Innovation within reach. [Blog post]. *New York Times*. Retrieved from opinionator.blogs.nytimes.com /2014/08/21/innovation-within-reach/?_r=0

Think Like an Architect, Draw Like an Engineer

by Erin Riley

Experience: Intermediate
Age group: 12–15 (8th grade)
Group size: 12–18
Time: 5–7 days, 50-minute sessions
Materials: LEGO bricks, doors, and windows; foamcore; guidelines; digital camera; standard quad and isometric paper; mechanical pencils, fine-point graphics pens, and colored paper; architectural drawing reference page; sticky notes

Figure 22.1: Bricks are clumped by color.

This unit was designed for an eighth-grade art elective at Greenwich Academy, in Greenwich, Connecticut, exploring the intersection of building, 2D and 3D visualization, and representation through drawing. The original idea for this project was inspired by a conversation with Colin Callahan at St. Paul's School in Concord, New Hampshire, based on some of the school's wonderful work in its Architecture course. In this project, students build LEGO models, create multiview plans, and rebuild and review peer plans. The sequence of activities builds spatial skills and helps create a foundation for architectural and technical drawing as well as understanding points of view in CAD applications. The plan acts as a prototype, going through a peer review and revision process.

there are enough bricks for everyone. Other guidelines include a projection, windows, and doors so structures have a baseline level of complexity (fig. 22.3).

Students hand in their buildings. They will take 360-degree photographs of the structures in the next class.

Lesson sequence

Day 1: Exploration with building

I store the bricks in a huge utility bin and the first order of business is to clump the bricks by color (fig. 22.1). I couple this organizational moment with a day of building and playing.

Days 2 and 3: Build a four-sided structure

Students are given a piece of foamcore for a base and set of guidelines. They choose their brick color and start working. The guidelines (fig. 22.2)[1] place constraints on the building size to ensure

```
                    TODAY
         BUILD A FOUR-SIDED STRUCTURE

                 GUIDELINES:
                  FOUR SIDES
            14 X 14 X 8 UNITS
                MAXIMUM DIMENSIONS

              1 UNIT =

                 MONOCHROME
     AT LEAST ONE SIDE MUST HAVE A PROJECTION
     HAVE AT LEAST ONE DOOR AND ONE WINDOW
               MUST BE STABLE
       MUST HAVE A CLEAR INTERIOR SPACE

             SOME SUGGESTIONS...
       PLAN A FOOTPRING... MAYBE USE GRAPH PAPER?
          OFF-SET BRICKS FOR STABILITY...
         FIND THE OUTSIDE DIMENSIONS FIRST...
                     COUNT!
```

Figure 22.2:
Guidelines are provided.

Figure 22.3: Each structure requires a baseline level of complexity.

Day 4: Thinking in three dimensions—isometric drawing

This is an exploration day. Students are given isometric drawing paper and asked to create free-form drawings based on a cube unit. They are asked to identify X, Y, and Z planes and differentiate the planes with shading or color (fig. 22.4).

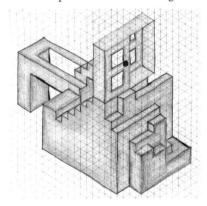

Figure 22.4: Freeform isometric drawing.

During this period students also take turns photographing their work in 360 degrees.[2] The photos are uploaded into a master class folder in Google Drive. Builders compare the final peer-built piece to the photographs.

Days 5 and 6: Make the building plan

Students have access to standard quad and isometric graph paper[3] as well as mechanical pencils, fine-point graphics pens, and colored pencils to represent their building (figs. 22.5a, b). I supply an architectural drawing reference page that can guide them in representing floor plans, elevations, sections, and isometric views.

At this point, if you have students who are done with their drawing (while others are still working) and you have access to a large format printer, you can print 18 × 24 inch isometric paper. This is an excellent lesson in scale.

Days 7 and 8: Switch and build

The original builder takes apart his or her creation and hands the pieces to a peer builder/reviewer. The peer builder builds according to the plan (fig. 22.6). Once finished, the 360-degree view is shared, and the peer reviews the plan by adding suggestions and improvement ideas to sticky notes (fig. 22.7).

Figure 22.6: Peer builders attempt to build according to the plan.

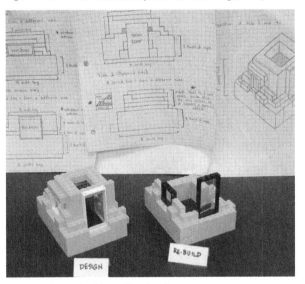

Figure 22.7: Peer builders offer ideas for improvement.

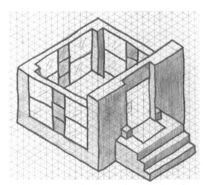

Figure 22.5: Building plan
a: On isometric paper
b: On graph paper

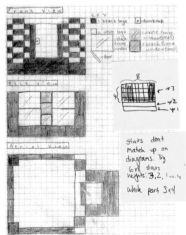

Day 9: Revision and reflection

Peer-build and revision suggestions are returned to the original builders. Students make final revisions, followed by class reflection and sharing.

Resources and tips

- **Slideshow.** This slideshow shows different ways building plans can be represented.[4]
- **LEGO pieces.** I used one box of LEGO Basic Bricks Deluxe[5] per three students and three boxes of LEGO Doors and Windows[6] for the class.
- **Storage.** I store the bricks in a large bin and stash it safely away from other LEGO pieces and robotics parts.
- **Good reading.** Excellent article on the importance of teaching drawing to develop spatial skills for art and technical fields: Sorby, S. A. (1999). Developing 3D spatial skills. *Engineering Design Graphics Journal*, 63(2), 21–32.[7]

Notes

1. fablearn.stanford.edu /fellows/MeaningfulMaking /IDBBuildingGuidelines.pdf
2. drive.google.com/folderview?id= oBzgKKl57Qs_bSDJSVGtMalpmaG8
3. Printable isometric graph paper: fablearn.stanford.edu/fellows /MeaningfulMaking/iso.pdf
4. docs.google.com/presentation /d/1gnyacDkCH5E6dSfNs5y4adxf DRTuWYoCuaYaNAhnfSo
5. shop.lego.com/en-US/LEGO-Basic-Bricks -Deluxe-6177
6. shop.lego.com/en-US/LEGO-Doors -Windows-6117
7. edgj.org/index.php/EDGJ/article /viewFile/126/122

Drawing: A Visual Language for Makers

by Erin Riley

Drawing is like writing using pictures instead of words. It is a form of communication that can be useful, expressive, descriptive, and observational. It gives form to visual ideas. Including drawing as part of the process of making things is fun and provides a good framework for understanding 2D and 3D design.

Drawing approaches

The following is a list of drawing approaches that are used most in the Engineering and Design Lab.

1. Orthographic projection

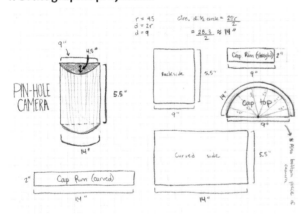

Figure 23.1: Orthographic projection of a pinhole camera.

Orthographic projection presents multiple 2D views of a 3D object. It's used in architecture and engineering (fig. 23.1). Critical information could include measurements, part names, or notes about the object. This type of drawing is an excellent exercise leading up to 3D modeling. It provides a framework for students to understand how to work around a three-dimensional object.

2. Isometric projection

Isometric projection is artificial 3D representation using X, Y, and Z axes and 120-degree angles to produce a 2D picture that looks 3D (fig. 23.2). It's great for communicating 3D ideas quickly

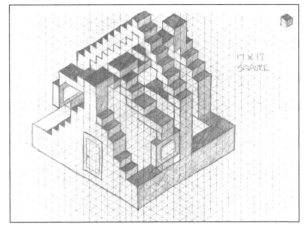

Figure 23.2: Isometric projection of a LEGO build.

and an excellent precursor to linear perspective. The artist MC Escher used it in optical illusions.

3. Building plans

Building plans can include all of the above. Examples would be LEGO kit instructions or IKEA furniture assembly plans.

4. Mind map

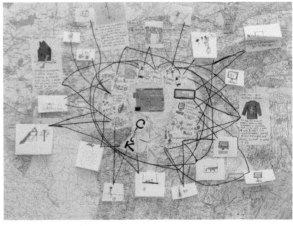

Figure 23.3: Arduino Mind Map project.

Mind maps express how ideas connect in graphical form. An example assignment is the Arduino Mind Map project (fig. 23.3).[1] Students are asked to create a mind map to brainstorm all the possible projects and inventions to build using an Arduino microcontroller.

5. Descriptive drawing

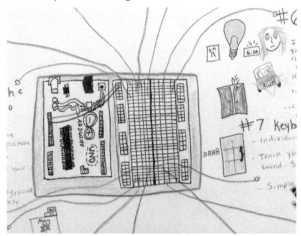

Figure 23.4: Descriptive drawing of an Arduino microcontroller and breadboard.

This kind of drawing is very useful as a record of your observations. Think Lewis and Clark journey log[2] or Albertus Seba's *Cabinet of Natural Curiosities*.[3] Annotate with notes for even more detail (fig. 23.4). Descriptive drawing is great for a sketchbook[4] or journal entry.

6. Schematics

Schematics are drawings of systems using symbols such as a subway map or circuit diagram.

Drawing materials and tools

A lot of the drawing that happens in the lab is preparatory work for 2D and 3D design for fabrication. Precision matters here so students need access to good measuring and drafting tools such as the following:

- Calipers
- Tape measures
- Different types of rulers (clear, cork bottom, various sizes)
- T-squares
- 45/90 and 30/60 triangles
- Compasses
- Drawing paper
- Different types of graph paper (Cartesian, dot, isometric)[5]
- Graphite and colored pencils
- Sharpies
- Grey graphic pens
- Brush markers
- Industrial pencil sharpener

More thoughts on drawing

Makers who develop skills in drawing feel confident about representing their ideas visually. Whether they are communicating an idea for self-expression or for a technical end, these drawing methods can work together and provide powerful tools for bringing one's imagination into the world. There are many more types of drawing than those listed above, and ultimately we develop hybrid styles that best reflect what we are trying to communicate.

Notes

1. Student handout for Arduino Mind Map project: fablearn.stanford.edu/fellows /MeaningfulMaking/ArduinoMindMap.pdf
2. nationalgeographic.com/lewisandclark /journey_intro.html
3. taschen.com/pages/en/catalogue/classics /all/44913/facts.seba_cabinet_of_natural _curiosities.htm
4. Examples of student sketchbooks and journals erinriley.weebly.com/making -books.html
5. Different types of printable graph paper: printablepaper.net/category/graph

Cyanotype Blueprints

by Erin Riley

Experience: Intermediate
Age group: 10–14
Group size: 12–18
Hours: 8 days; 40-minute periods

This project was designed for sixth-grade students at Greenwich Academy in Greenwich, Connecticut, to bring together ideas from history, art, science, and technology. In history class, students study world religions and do research on significant buildings within religious traditions. In art class they make drawings from architectural plans of the historic building. In the Engineering and Design Lab, they make blueprints of their buildings using an old-fashioned photographic printing process called *cyanotype*, which creates the distinctive blue lines.

Leading up to the project

Before the blueprint project, a joint art project with art and technology helped the students gain an understanding of 2D-design space and vector drawing, an essential lab skill for digital fabrication. Students created geometric collage designs that they translated into vector designs using the pen tool in Adobe Illustrator. These were made into linoleum block prints in art class (fig. 24.1).

The goals for the project included the following:
- To integrate history, art, science, and technology
- To explore the science and art of sacred geometry
- To learn how to make cyanotype blueprints
- To use graphic tools and drawing
- To use 2D and 3D design for fabrication

Figure 24.1: Linoleum block prints.

The sequence in Studio Art and the Engineering and Design Lab

1. **Sketching.** Students spend one class period exploring making shapes in their sketchbooks with graphic tools like triangles, compasses, and rulers (fig. 24.2).

Figure 24.2: Sketching architectural shapes.

2. **Creating a floor plan.** The structures they research in history become a springboard for a newly interpreted floor plan in graphite. Art

students are encouraged to pull out the shapes and profiles that are most appealing visually to create a design.

3. **Masking.** In the cyanotype process, an acetate mask is created to block the sun from reaching parts of paper. Using 2D vector software, the students design shapes, which are cut on the vinyl cutter. These shapes can be combined with tape to create a mask design (fig. 24.3).

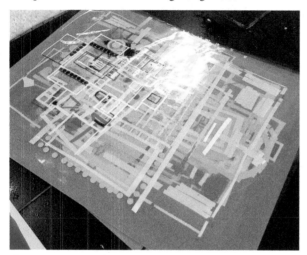

Figure 24.3: Acetate shapes cut on the vinyl cutter.

4. **Cyanotype process.** Students mix up the cyanotype chemicals, treat the paper, and expose their designs to twenty minutes of winter sun (fig. 24.4). The masked area remains white while the exposed area turns blue.

Figure 24.4: Cyanotype designs reacting to sunlight.

5. **Finishing.** Rinse and dry the prints (fig. 24.5).

Figure 24.5: Finished designs.

What followed

The cyanotype blueprints provided a framework for students' understanding of basic CAD drawing principles of 2D–3D through the representation of the floor plan. In the next project, they built the footprint of their designs with the 3D software SketchUp using the Push/Pull tool to create their 3D models.

Where Is the Line?
Telegraph Construction with Specific Instructions

by Heather Allen Pang

Every teacher in every classroom contemplating a project plan faces the question of how much guidance, how many constraints, and how much help to give students. I have been thinking about this problem for projects where the content is specific, for example, the invention of the telegraph and the beginning of the revolution in communication and technology that brought us the cell phones we now take for granted. I have also been thinking about the larger question of the role of kits in teaching and learning.

I have no problem with skill building, such as teaching a specific skill like soldering or formatting of a bibliography with specific teacher instructions. Students will do these tasks many times, and learning to do them the right way is not a moment for individual exploration. If everyone solders in their own way, people get hurt and connections do not get made. If everyone formats their bibliography in their own way, then it is not really a bibliography, and students do not get to participate in the scholarship of history.

At the other end of the spectrum, there are times when I want students to have free range about what they do or how they show that they have mastered some subject or task, and the only constraints I might impose are time and materials. Students can design any kind of monument they think represents the woman they pick, they may write any type of reflection (poetry, prose, fiction, nonfiction) in response to their reading of a historical novel, and when they pick a nineteenth-century technology to explain to the class, they can do whatever they think will help their classmates understand.

Most projects, however, are not that simple. I spent some time at Constructing Modern Knowledge (CMK) summer institute[1] during the summer of 2014 learning to build a telegraph. And it worked, sort of. (Dots were good, but the dashes tended to get stuck.) I am planning on having pairs of students build telegraphs that will allow them to send their dots and dashes from one end of the classroom to the other, and maybe farther. At CMK part of my challenge was finding the right parts and hand making the wooden base. But at school, I precut the bases on the laser cutter; that is a good use of my time and a very bad use of student time.

Then things get tricky. Having the students only follow my instructions and put together what I have assembled inhibits their learning. If I hand them a base and tell them to search the Internet for instructions on how to make a telegraph and then have them search all over school for the right kinds of magnetic metals, iron nails, the right size covered wire, etc., how much of the learning is about the technology and how much is about bothering the maintenance staff and running around frustrated?

After spending a bit of time pondering this, I decided that I would start someplace in the middle and try it, and then ask the students what they learned, what they liked, and what might make the lesson better. I will provide the supplies but not sort them out into kits, and links to basic instructions[2] along with a brief framework of the historical circumstances of the invention as it happened in the nineteenth century. Students will take it from there.

I started with a design meeting with Angi Chau, our lab director, and Diego Fonstad, our tinkerer in residence. (Yes, I know I am extremely lucky to work at a school with both of these people.) We tried a few variations and settled on a base for the key, a base for the receiver, and the different types of wire we would have the students use. We cut the base parts out of wood on the laser cutter to make things go more quickly. Diego figured out that metal brads worked best as fasteners. Angi wrote out the instructions, and we shared those with the students.

I put the girls in pairs, showed them the supplies (fig. 25.1), and told them to follow the instructions. I added a rule they already knew: before they ask me a question, they have to show me where they are on the instructions document. Most of their questions can be answered by figuring out where they are on the instructions document.

Figure 25.1: Supplies, not kits.

We were trying to use up some wire we had in the lab, so the first thing they had to do was untwist it. That was both fun and frustrating. Some girls were much better at it than others. Some observations:

- Wire strippers are hard to use. A student who is rarely an expert in history turned out to be a pro at stripping wire.
- It was not clear to all students that the connections had to be metal touching metal for the telegraph to work (fig. 25.2).

Figure 25.2: Making connections.

- Following instructions is not easy.

At the end of the first fifty-minute period a student said, "Mrs. Pang, this project is fun! It is really hard, but it is fun." (It was as if she was channeling Seymour Papert's concept of "hard fun." I wish I had that on video.)

Most students finished the basic build early on day two but then had to start troubleshooting since very few of the telegraphs worked on the first try (fig. 25.3). I don't know if we struck exactly the right balance of instruction versus exploration, but the lesson did achieve several of my goals:

- The students created a working telegraph and demonstrated an understanding of how the nineteenth-century version worked.
- They had the chance to troubleshoot their own creation with almost no help other than to remind them to check connections and keep trying.
- Our conversation about invention, the role of instant communication in the nineteenth and twentieth centuries and how much we take it for granted, was rich and thoughtful.

Figure 25.3: "It works!"

The student reflections highlighted the importance of checking the connections, how hard it is to untangle wire, and how wire strippers work. These lessons are not part of the history curriculum, but they are certainly part of life's curriculum.

Notes

1. constructingmodernknowledge.com
2. fablearn.stanford.edu/fellows /MeaningfulMaking/MakeaTelegraph.pdf

Eighth Graders Design Monuments to Historic Figures

by Heather Allen Pang

Figure 26.1: A completed monument model.

For several years, I have ended eighth-grade history with a project that brings together two themes we have looked at through the year: individuals who make a difference and historical monuments. The students have finished their research and class presentations on the 1950s, 1960s, 1970s, and 1980s. They pick one of the important women, or women's issues, from their group research projects and design and build a model of a monument to a person that they would like to see on the National Mall in Washington, DC (fig. 26.1). I only grade the presentation to the class, not the monument itself. The students need to be able to explain how the parts of the monument would make a visitor feel and learn, how the monument reflected the life and values of the person, and how their design and building process had worked.

These presentations on the last day of school are a fantastic way to hear from the students, and they enjoy the chance to show off their work. We don't do a peer critique at that point because the year is over; they couldn't change anything.

After they have picked their subject from the work they had already done on women in the twentieth century, I tell them to think big but to keep in mind that they would have to figure out how to build the model of the monument. They have two weeks in the lab to design and build the models.

When I designed the project, I had two goals. The first was to create an engaging, thoughtful, and challenging project on which to end the year thinking about important themes from their studies. The second was to stretch students to think more critically about using history to become the active designers of historical works rather than consumers of other people's created histories. This project achieved those goals. It also presented some new challenges for the preparations I needed to make for the students to engage in this type of historical practice. We also have a great deal of fun.

I was asked by a prospective parent who came into the lab while we were working why we would take so much time from "real history" to build things. The question is an important one, and I described some of my observations to the visitor. Students were debating the merits of representing historical events literally or metaphorically. They had long discussions about the need to include negative information in a monument for historical accuracy. They discussed the need to present their subject as a hero, a role model without flaws. They had delved deeply into their historical knowledge to find ways to show a modern visitor the historical realities of the lives of their subjects. I had seen more "real" historical thinking in the project up to that point than even I had expected.

This project brings together several threads from the eighth-grade year, including the ways we memorialize history, the importance of women in American history, and the ways in which students are themselves practicing historians, not just consumers of information. The students used the tools in the fab lab at school to realize their designs, primarily the laser cutter, the foam cutter, and the 3D printer.

Figure 26.2: The model includes the monument and the surrounding area.

This project requires students to think about which important aspects of their subject they want to show in the monument, how literal or symbolic they want their monument to be, and how to design the best user experience (fig. 26.2). It also requires them to do a great deal of math to get the right proportions and scale (fig. 26.3). All group projects require collaboration, but one of the benefits of building something physical turns out that it is much harder for a student to hide and let her classmates do all the work. It also requires a different kind of collaboration because no one is sure of the "right" thing to do.

Figure 26.3: Planning and measuring.

After the students had successfully presented the projects to the class, we talked about the challenges of the project. Some of these challenges are the same in any group project: time management, delegation of work to group members, and resolving differences of opinion about creative or technical issues. But they also talked about challenges that only came from actually building their monument models, or that came out very differently because of the making process.

First they talked about skills: they had to learn new software and improve their skills on the machines in the lab, which are important challenges in their learning process. These challenges brought out leadership in some students in ways

that other settings had not. They also talked about the interdisciplinary nature of the project, not the way teachers sometimes do, fitting one subject into another because it is a current trend, but authentically, because they could not possibly build what they imagined without using math. They talked about working out issues of scale and understanding how people would react to their presentation of historical material in physical and symbolic ways. The students also talked about how to take an idea ("What if we had lights on our fountain?") through the process of design and creation.

Other students described the benefits of doing a new type of project. They acknowledged that they had to think through what an architect thinks about, for example, thinking about a fountain going down into the ground rather than at ground level and how they would build that. They had to think about constraints; for example, they couldn't just put up a façade without thinking about struts for supporting the façade and how that might work for someone visiting the monument. My favorite comment was "Something that's unexpected during building can actually work out!"

Bringing fabrication tools into the history class opens up ideas about the role of making in all academic subjects. When students experience history through the process of fabrication, they become historians and have to come to a deep understanding of their subject. This opens up a wider variety of project-based learning for social studies and humanities classes, and brings students and teachers more options for creativity and deeper investigation of core academic topics and skills.

This project also reflects an ongoing and evolving interdisciplinary collaboration among Yvette Yamagata, the algebra teacher; Angi Chau, director of the fab lab; and me.

Each year I have increased the connections with math topics. We noticed the scale issues, and the students did too, so now I work with Yvette; she designs some indirect measurement activities to support the project. When we go to see the monuments in Washington, DC, the students do indirect measurements and record their data in their journals, and we save that material for the spring project. We also have them record their reactions to different monuments in terms of the scale, structure, and style of the places they visit. They will have already done a sample activity measuring buildings on campus.

The idea came from some of the students, who realized that if they wanted to know how a thirty-foot-tall monument would look (fig. 26.4), they needed to find something that was thirty feet tall and stand next to it. They started out measuring the lab itself to compare, but I like the idea of building the measurement process into the curriculum and so does the math teacher. In addition, the math teacher has come down to the lab, observed the students doing the scaling, and intervened in their discussions or pushed their thinking a bit further. The students have been creative about how they tried to imagine scale; we don't want to interrupt that process, but we do want them to apply skills they have learned in other places.

to expand what we think of as history instruction and introduce students to how the work of historians happens in our culture. After building their own monument prototypes, students are more likely to think critically about historical monuments they see, and they are more likely to feel that they have the ability to present historical material in creative ways (fig. 26.5). Doing history in the lab fosters making, and making in the lab makes them better historians.

Figure 26.5: The monument project has a student doing the work of a historian, not just learning about history.

Figure 26.4: Dealing with scale.

The collaboration with Angi in the fab lab has been a huge part of the project. I developed it with Diego Fonstad, our tinkerer in residence, and refined it the next year with Angi. The girls get more comfortable asking for help and working together with another expert adult in the room, and that allows for greater creativity. Students who want to go further with one of the tools can do so since sometimes Angi is able to spend significant time with one group, working on some technical challenge; that would not be possible without two people in the lab at least some of the time.

Bringing history class down to the fab lab to build monuments is one more tool we can use

Silhouettes: Old and New Technology of Portraits

by Heather Allen Pang

While I was thinking about a simple laser-cut project to teach the Inkscape software and how to use the laser cutter in my eighth-grade history class, I happened upon two things at about the same time. One was a blog post by Sylvia Martinez about starting the year with making,[1] and the other was the image of a page of silhouettes of the family of John Quincy Adams.[2] I decided to start with the students themselves, using new tools to create an old-fashioned silhouette or profile.

The process starts with a backlit photo taken in a dark room against a light curtain. (I taped paper on the window in my classroom.) The photo needs to be edited in basic editing software to make it a black-and-white image against an even lighter background. This introduced the students to the photo editing tools they all had on their devices but many had never explored. Importing the photo into Inkscape using the paint bucket tool to fill the shape of the head and deleting the fill, leaving only the stroke line, creates a clear vector line for the laser cutter.

The students enjoyed creating their profiles, even as they expressed some frustration with the tools,[3] but these challenges allowed for some useful discussion about how to figure out what had gone wrong and how to troubleshoot the technology and our projects. They learned several of the editing tools in Inkscape, and they will be well prepared to do more complicated projects using the software later in the year. These are all things I expected to come out of the project.

What I was not so sure about was how well they would see the historical issues involved, but I should not have worried. I showed them the John Adams profiles and several other late eighteenth- and early-nineteenth-century examples, and then we talked about what it cost to have a profile cut (25 cents for two copies in 1808, according to one

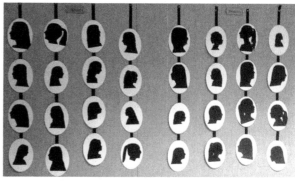

Figure 27.1: Completed student silhouettes hanging in the classroom.

source), and why these images were so popular. They could clearly see how important it would be to families to have an image of a loved one, especially if part of the family were moving away or going to war. They talked about how many photos we have today and how different it would be not to have those images to look at. We also talked about when photography was invented and when it became available to ordinary people. In the course of a short discussion we covered economics, settlement patterns, and the human desire to have images of ourselves—not bad for a simple laser-cut project.

I hung the silhouettes on the wall of the classroom (fig. 27.1), and the students had fun recognizing themselves and their friends. At back-to-school night the parents loved seeing their own children, and I had to laugh at the sight of them using their smartphones to take photos of the silhouettes, somehow bringing the idea full circle and proving the point that today we cannot possibly have enough images of ourselves or our children.

Notes

1. sylviamartinez.com/back-to-school-start
2. masshist.org/database/767
3. Inkscape is sometimes difficult to download and install on a Mac, and if the image is not dark enough, the shape will not be not clear.

28 Story Architects: Reflection on an Integrated Project

by Erin Riley

Figure 28.1: Story architects at work.

Sarah Holzschuh's senior English class, New York State of Mind, at Greenwich Academy in Greenwich, Connecticut, worked in the Engineering and Design Lab on a two-week interdisciplinary project bringing together the concepts explored in literature and translating these ideas into the visual language of architecture. Students selected one of six texts they had studied throughout the year, and over the course of several class periods worked to construct a building model based on the themes, character trajectories, or the experience of reading the work they'd chosen (fig. 28.1). Inspiration for the collaboration came from a project between Creative Writing and Architecture graduate students at Columbia University.[1]

Lesson sequence

Day 1: Design challenge and exploration of materials
Before being introduced to the Story Architect project, students were given a one-day design

challenge to create a carport for a toy car (fig. 28.2). This activity was specifically designed to get the students thinking about scale and the nature of the materials they were using from both an engineering and aesthetic perspective. This challenge also offered them time for exploration and reflection within the group. The solutions were varied, and the students were inspired by the wide range of visual and structural possibilities with cardboard, tape, and translucent materials.

Figure 28.2: Carport design challenge.

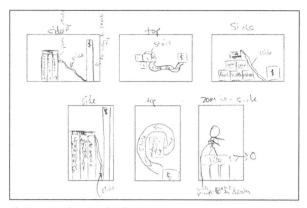

Figure 28.3: Planning sketches.

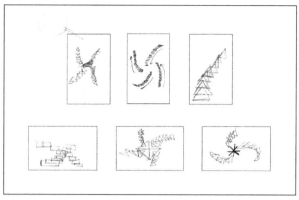

Figure 28.4: Thumbnails.

Day 2: Book selection and thumbnails

After being introduced to the Story Architects concept, students took time for written exploration, reflecting on a series of questions designed to get them thinking about literary concepts in structural terms. The students then created a series of thumbnails, quickly sketching visual ideas from the book they had chosen (figs. 28.3 and 28.4). Many students moved on to a more detailed thumbnail in preparation for building.

Days 3–5: Building

Each class had three days to build their structures. Guidelines were loose; they were given an 8 × 8 inch laser-cut platform to build the structure and could expand the air space to fit within a 10 × 10 envelope. Their only other limitation was a designated collection of building materials, including cardboard, wooden dowels, and transparent and translucent paper (figs. 28.5). The class was familiar with the materials, having used them in their one-day carport challenge.

City Planning

Students put forth proposals for how to organize the structures for the final exhibition. They ultimately decided on a grouping of structures into "neighborhoods" organized by book. Negative space pockets were engraved on the ShopBot to create the foundations for each building. The students built their structures on 8 × 8 platforms that fit into the foundations for the gallery installation (fig. 28.6).

Student Reflections

After the installation, student writer/architects explained their process and design choices. Here's one:

> At its core Colum McCann's *Let the Great World Spin* is a book about hope. While the immediately apparent themes in the novel seem to be hardship, loss, filth, and destitution, there are continually moments in which the characters find happiness and light in the midst of all the darkness. My architectural piece is an attempt to emphasize the importance and centrality of the characters' search for something beautiful in their lives.

Figure 28.5: Building stories.

Figure 28.6: City structures installed in the Luchsender Gallery.

At the base of the structure, there are many short buildings of various heights, seemingly oppressed by three taller buildings in the center. Some of the small buildings are broken, missing large pieces from their sides, whereas some are even collapsing onto each other. None of these buildings have roofs for coverage and protection. These structures are symbolic of the difficult situations that many of the characters find themselves in during the novel.

The most important part of the piece, however, is the beams that connect these buildings to each other, as well as to the increasingly taller buildings in the center. These beams symbolize the ability of anyone to move away from the darkness and find moments of joy or happiness in their lives. The rising beams represent the characters' ability to "rise" up from their situation and find beauty in their lives, if even for a short time. The beams also reflect Phillipe Petit's tightrope walk between the Twin Towers, which is a recurrent theme in the novel. I think that Petit's tightrope walk is so central to this book because most of the characters find themselves in horrible situations that they cannot control, whereas Petit places himself in a dangerous situation by choice and ultimately makes something beautiful out of it instead of focusing on the danger or potential outcome of his endeavors.

The three taller buildings in the center of the piece represent the happiness and light that the characters can find in their lives if they simply look for it. The area higher up is less crowded, and the buildings are covered by roofs, which represents a safer and more protected place. In this piece my goal was to create a structure that would reflect the hope in this novel and focus on the search for occasional happiness instead of oppression by constant sadness. (Katie S.)

Reflection

After the first experience with this project, Sarah Holzschuh and I continued to develop and improve Story Architects. Our goal is to enrich students' experience as learners. We hope that their understanding of literature is enhanced by the opportunity to express ideas through making and designing an artifact that has personal meaning to them. Built into this experience were design and structural challenges that students solved with limited resources and time (fig. 28.7).

Figure 28.7: The Story Architects project continues to develop.

The project itself is an ongoing prototype, and the collaboration we have forged is the start of what we hope will continue to grow with our students. This group was particularly interesting to study. Not only was it the students' final year at Greenwich Academy, but this class contained some of the original members from the inaugural year of the Middle School FLL Robotics team. Since then, STEAM education and curricular integration of "making," engineering, and design into every girl's experience at the school has gained institutional support. Throughout the course of their education, all of the students will continue to get a rich experience with the visual arts, woodworking, computer programming, physical computing, electronics, 2D- and 3D-digital design and fabrication, and the engineering design process. This project will undoubtedly evolve as

students will be able to draw upon more tools and experiences in the Engineering and Design Lab in their time at Greenwich Academy.

Story Architects 2.0

Sarah and I collaborated on a second version of Story Architects the following semester. The concept of mapping was introduced, and a large-scale map was printed and installed in the gallery. Students identified a location for their structure using map pins and string (fig. 28.8). Material choices expanded with the second iteration of the project, and a wider variety of design ideas was evident (figs. 28.9 and 28.10).

Note

1. opinionator.blogs.nytimes.com/2013/08/03/writers-as-architects

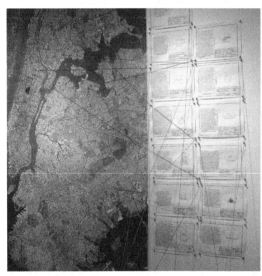

Figure 28.8: Mapping structures.

Figure 28.9: Additional material choices.

Figure 28.10: Wider variety of story structures design.

29

The Techno Ugly Christmas Sweater Project

by Mark Schreiber

Figure 29.1: Modeling my "ugly" Christmas sweater.

Ugly Christmas sweaters are pretty hip these days. Wal-Mart sells them, Target sells them, and there's even a shop in my town where you can "uglify" your very own Christmas sweater. And yes, we have an ugly sweater contest at our school (that I plan on winning by the way). In 2014, I made a pretty nifty one (fig. 29.1), and as I write this article my advanced engineering class is pushing toward the completion of some pretty sophisticated ugly sweaters. Some blink, some play music, some even look like the Griswolds' house in *National Lampoon's Christmas Vacation*. One has car horns on it and yet another a Christmas trivia tree!

One might ask, "Why would you do such a project?", and I might answer with a Christmas quote like "Bah humbug!"

The truth is that this has been an *illuminating* project. Students, driven by the desire to create something amazing, have learned so much.

MaKey MaKey, Soundplant, Scratch programming, more Arduino lines of code than I can count, flashy LEDs, e-textiles, laser cutting, soldering—I could go on and on. The room is abuzz with excitement—the warm smells of gingerbread being cut on the laser cutter fill the air, sound bites of Christmas music and movie clips playing in the background, and students helping each other troubleshoot their projects.

A simple techno ugly Christmas sweater

Materials

- A really ugly sweater
- A laptop
- A MaKey MaKey, conductive ornaments, or other conductive bling
- Craft and decorative materials such as Christmas décor items and cotton-ball snow
- Optional: LEDs and batteries, LilyPad, Gemma, or other small sewable microcontrollers

Instructions

1. Download Soundplant or use Scratch to map keyboard keys to sound clips, songs, and such (see Resources below).

2. Lay out your sweater and glue conductive elements to the front.

3. Turn your sweater inside out and mount a MaKey MaKey inside. Run wires to each conductive element on the front of your sweater. (Just duct tape them to the inside since this is probably temporary.)

4. Link your favorite audio clips or songs to the A, S, D, F, W, space, and arrow keys in SoundPlant or in Scratch.

5. Connect yourself to the MaKey MaKey ground. (You can use an alligator clip running down the sleeve to a ring, metal bracelet, watch, etc.)

6. Test your sweater. It should play clips or music when you touch the various conductive elements on the sweater.

7. Decorate your sweater to make it earn the "ugly" label.

8. Go mobile! To make sure your laptop doesn't go to sleep when the lid is shut, keep it attached to the MaKey MaKey with SoundPlant or Scratch open, and put it in a Christmas gift bag. Run the USB cord inside the sweater, and add some gift tissue to the gift bag to hide the laptop.

9. Optional: To add twinkle, add some LEDs or blinky LEDs with a LilyPad or Gemma. Cotton balls make nice "snow" and diffuse the light very well while hiding the LEDs.

Advanced ugly sweater with an Arduino-timed light display

The core of this project[1] is a sequencer called Vixen, an AdaFruit Flora (with a FastLED library), and a bunch of NeoPixel strips (or other digitally addressable RGB LEDs). Grab a gift bag, load your laptop, some speakers, and tissue paper, and you are all set!

First, pick a theme. Let's use the film *Frozen* as an example. I used the free version of WavePad to edit the *Frozen* theme song to a shorter length. I loaded the code on my Flora so that it could receive serial communications from Vixen, set up the NeoPixel elements for the different zones of my sweater, and then imported the song into Vixen.

Suggested materials
Flora, Neopixels, wire, cotton balls, laser-cut snowflakes, ugly-sweater bling

Instructions
1. Download and install software: Adafruit's Arduino IDE, FAST LED library, and Vixen (see Resources below).

2. Upload sketch to Flora. (Remember USBTiny-ISP programmer and your COM port.)

3. Close out of Arduino IDE.

4. Configure Vixen for generic serial port using the same COM port that the Flora used (see Resources below).

5. Set up Vixen displays. You may wish to break your full strand of NeoPixels into small sections so that you can create different effects on each one. I used about 80 pixels on my sweater with eight different segments (also called elements in Vixen).

6. Connect the NeoPixels to Pin6, Ground, and VBatt on the Flora. (Make sure you put a 330-ohm resistor on the data pin of the first pixel so you don't blow that pixel and kill the entire setup.)

7. Close Vixen and the Flora.

8. Plug in the Flora connected to the Neopixels. You should see a green light and yellow RX LED on the Flora flash.

9. Open Vixen. (You should now see a solid yellow light on Flora if all is configured correctly; if not, make sure that your display is set up to receive the same COM port as the Flora is using.)

10. Open a New Sequence-Timed Sequence in Vixen.

11. Drag an effect to the pixel segment that you'd like to test, and click the Play arrow (green Play button). You can use the "chase" effect to test the whole strip at once.

12. Build your sweater: Cut strip into segments, run wires, and resolder to chain the strip segments all the way around the sweater to different locations. (Suggestion: Start at the bottom left, then go up the side of the zipper, around the collar, down the other side of the zipper to the bottom, up to the left middle, to the left pocket, and finally around the back to the right pocket.) You can power pixels from anywhere—the beginning, the middle, or the end (or all of them); just make sure your data pin wire is one continuous strip.

13. Test it again. Once the strips are installed on the sweater, check all connections and retest.

14. Take a gingerbread break.

15. Sync music to the lights in Vixen audio track. (Warning: This can take a long time!)

16. Decorate and camouflage the LEDs with cotton balls, laser-cut felt, or other fun stuff.

17. Tweak, troubleshoot, and repeat.

18. Hook it all up to your computer, hide your computer in a gift bag, put on your sweater, and head out to your Ugly Sweater Christmas party (fig. 29.2).

Figure 29.2: An ugly Christmas sweater complete with gift bag sound system.

Resources

Simply ugly sweater

MaKey MaKey[2] plus **Soundplant**.[3] This combination is the one-two punch of an awesome interactive ugly sweater. For extra effects, put in two MaKey MaKeys (just reprogram the keyboard map on one of them). If you are using a Mac, you might want to download the NoSleep app. This way you can close the Mac and still have it run Soundplant.

To add some basic twinkle: Adafruit's Gemma[4] or SparkFun's LilyPad[5] or Tiny LilyPad. The Adafruit sequin hat tutorial will help you get started.

Advanced ugly sweater

Vixen plus **Arduino**. The Vixen software[6] controls the RGB LED strips.[7] Upload the code to Adafruit's Flora e-textile board (just make sure you have the FAST LED library installed). Vixen is only available for Windows (but can run on Mac using a virtual system). This project works with an Arduino Uno, but if you use an AdaFruit Flora,[8] you can go mobile.

For the sound, use the WavePad sound editor, a slim sound-editing tool. Get the free trial version.[9] SoundCloud[10] offers songs and sound effects to use with your project.

Notes

1. Ugly sweater video tutorial: youtu.be /fo9d0oDjQAY
2. makeymakey.com
3. soundplant.org
4. adafruit.com
5. sparkfun.com
6. vixenlights.com
7. Instructions on how to get RGB LEDs strips running with Vixen blog.huntgang.com /2014/11/08/vixen-lights-3-x-arduino -pixel-controller-ws2812b
8. learn.adafruit.com/getting-started-with-flora
9. nch.com.au/wavepad
10. soundcloud.com

The Molds of Civilization

by Gilson Domingues and Pietro Domingues

Figure 30.1: Brick making in ancient Egypt.

Modern fabrication techniques such as 3D printing are not the only way to reliably create nearly identical objects. Even in ancient times people used molds to manufacture everything from jewelry to bricks (fig. 30.1). This article will introduce the molding process, including utility and the current methods used in this process, then share a step-by-step process for how to make these molds using silicone, a low-cost, reliable material.

Reproduction by molding

It would be very interesting to think about an object and have it magically appear; however, according to the laws of physics, objects and systems tend to disorganize themselves over time, rather than forming neat, well-defined shapes. When we want to make one single part, we can spend hours and hours, and it might even be pleasant to work on it. But what if we want to reproduce a large quantity of something, keeping the same quality without having to craft every one with the same care? This is a challenge that mankind has been facing for a long time.

To solve this problem, we can use molds. Molds are a cavity that can be filled with a pliable material or liquid. After the material solidifies, the object can be removed and the mold refilled again. Using this process, called *casting*, we obtain very similar solid parts.

An everyday example is making ice cubes. They are made by putting liquid water into an ice cube tray (the mold), and after some time in the freezer, they become solid cubes and can be removed from the tray. Since antiquity, mankind has been making products based on the molding process (fig. 30.2). Jewelry, weapons, domestic utensils, bricks, and tools were made this way, and sometimes still are (fig. 30.3). Currently, big industries as well as artisans still make products through molding and casting.

Figure 30.2: Ancient molding and casting. Museum of Anatolian Civilizations, Ankara, Turkey. Photos by Gilson Domingues.

Figure 30.3: Making bricks in molds, a process still used today.

How to make silicone molds

Silicone is an excellent material for a mold because it can be used to make objects with complex geometry at a low cost (fig. 30.4). While the words *silicone* and *silicon* look similar, they are very different. Silicon is an element found in nature and is often used in creating integrated circuits. Silicone is a synthetic polymer that contains silicon plus other ingredients and has some very useful properties. It is slippery, insulating, and nontoxic, which are all useful for mold making.

Figure 30.4: A variety of objects made in silicone molds.

Types of silicone

Silicone comes from the factory in a liquid state, and it is sold in small containers (1 liter or ¼ gallon). There are two kinds of silicone: white and brown. On the right side of figure 30.5 we can see white silicone, used to mold materials at room temperature. On the left is brown silicone, which is used for high-melting temperature materials.

Figure 30.5: Two types of silicone: brown (left) and white (right).

The two workpieces on the left in figure 30.6 are produced by melting different materials at high temperatures, then casting them in the brown silicone mold. The white piece is paraffin wax and the other is tin. The four workpieces on the right are made of plaster of paris (the white one) and resin (the other three). These were cast at room temperature in the white silicone mold.

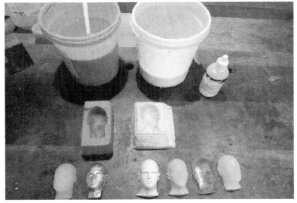

Figure 30.6: High-temperature molding (left) and low-temperature molding (right).

Materials needed

- Liquid silicone + catalyst
- A container to mix up the silicone
- A stirrer stick
- Another smaller container, to mix the silicone with catalyst (the leftover silicone will harden in this container, so use something that is disposable)

- Original workpiece (any kind of object you wish to reproduce, such as a 3D-printed part or a sculpture)

Instructions

1. Stir the silicone with a stick to ensure homogeneity. Then pour into a small container.

2. To start the solidification process, drop the catalyst (the right amount is usually indicated on the manual) into the silicone in the small container. Stir the mix completely for the recommended time.

3. Place the workpiece you want to reproduce in a container and pour the silicone over it. Fill so the workpiece is completely covered.

4. It may take from 30 minutes to many hours for the silicone to cure. (It depends on the amount of silicone.) To test, touch the silicone. If it sticks to your fingers, it is not cured yet.

5. When the silicone is cured, carefully remove the mold.

6. Now the mold is ready to use. Let us reproduce the workpiece!

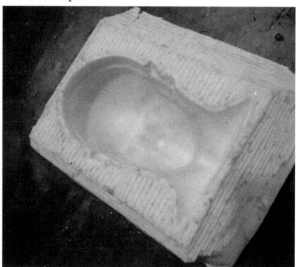

31

Reproducing Workpieces

by Gilson Domingues and Pietro Domingues

In the previous article we explained how to make silicone molds. In this article we will describe how to use these molds to reproduce workpieces using many different materials. This is a fast technique used to replicate complex parts that would take a long time to make with a 3D printer (fig. 31.1).

Figure 31.1: Objects of different materials cast from the same mold.

Some materials such as plaster of paris and polyester resin can be molded at room temperature. Other materials such as paraffin wax must be melted and poured into the molds. However, they do not require extremely high temperatures and can be melted on a stove or a Bunsen burner. Use of these materials is explained below.

Plaster of Paris

Materials needed
- Plaster (dry powder)
- Container
- Stick

Instructions

1. Mix water and dry plaster powder as directed in the instructions in a container. Stir the mix.

2. Drop the mixture into the mold. If necessary, force the mix against the mold to ensure that the mold is filled.

3. Plaster will be set after about 30 minutes. Then the workpiece is ready to remove.

Polyester Resin

Polyester resin is a great material for making low-cost, high-quality reproductions. Although the mechanical resistance of this material is not high, it can be used in some mechanical applications.

Polyester resin is often used by artisans to manufacture small objects like refrigerator magnets, miniatures, and keychains. As with silicone, resins are manufactured in a liquid state. A catalyst is used to change the liquid to a solid and give shape to the object.

WARNING: It's highly recommended to work in a place with fresh air, using gloves, glasses, and if possible, an air-purifying respirator.

Materials
- Resin (liquid)
- Catalyst (it comes with the resin)
- Small container

Instructions

1. Drop the resin and the catalyst in the container according to directions in the manual. Mix well.

2. Pour the resin into the mold.

3. Let the resin cure. It takes between 30 minutes and 2 hours, depending on climate conditions. When cured, remove from mold.

In this example, the resin was prepared without any pigment. As a result, the finished workpiece is transparent and has no color.

Adding color to resin

Pigment can be added to resin for the final product to have color. The pigment is manufactured as a paste (fig. 31.2) and added to the resin according to the concentration of the color desired (fig. 31.3). Then it is poured into the mold and cured using the same process described above (fig. 31.4).

Figure 31.2: Pigment paste for resin.   Figure 31.3: Add pigment to resin.

Figure 31.4: Pour pigmented resin in mold and remove finished workpiece when cured.

Modifying Resin

Resin can be modified by adding aggregates such as talcum powder, marble powder, or finely ground wood (called wood fiber or wood flour) (fig. 31.5). The addition of an aggregate modifies the viscosity of the liquid, changes the texture and color of the workpiece, and makes the resin go further. The difference between the two methods can be seen in figure 31.6. On the left, just resin was used; on the right, 30 percent talcum was added.

Figure 31.5: Adding talcum powder to resin mixture.   Figure 31.6: On the left, resin alone. On the right, resin with talcum powder added.

Figure 31.7: The red workpieces were 3D printed. The yellow ones are copies made from a mold.

Molding with modified resin is a fast technique used to replicate complex parts that would take a long time to make in a 3D printer. By making just one piece in the 3D printer, then making and using a mold of that piece, the reproduced workpieces look just like the 3D-printed one (fig. 31.7). In the figure, the red workpieces were 3D printed and used to make a mold. Then the yellow ones were cast from that mold. To prepare the 3D-printed pieces for mold making, we used spackling paste and sandpaper to obtain a smooth, flat surface.

In figure 31.8, the four parts of a gear cube design were replicated using the molding process. The gear cube assembly fit well and worked perfectly (fig. 31.9) and was created in much less time than it would take to 3D print the same object.

Figure 31.8: Gear cube parts made in a mold.

Figure 31.9: Assembled gear cube works perfectly.

Paraffin wax

Paraffin is derived from petroleum, and candles are made of paraffin. To get paraffin we can melt candles, but it is also available commercially in small grains (fig. 31.10). To mold with paraffin wax, it must be melted. The melting point of paraffin is relatively low, and it can be melted in a pan on a stove or over a Bunsen burner.

WARNING: Please wear protective clothing, shoes, and eyewear when using open flames.

Materials

- Paraffin
- Metal container or frying pan

Figure 31.10: Paraffin grains.

Instructions

Drop the paraffin into the metal container and heat it to 60°C (140°F). If using a frying pan, heat it carefully over a low flame. Avoid moving the pan abruptly, and do not put the paraffin directly on fire—it is flammable! If the paraffin catches fire, cover it with a lid larger in diameter than the pan.

The paraffin will slowly melt and turn clear.

After all the paraffin is melted, pour it carefully into the mold. The solidification is slow; it takes 15 to 45 minutes depending on the size of the workpiece. As the material solidifies, it will return to an opaque appearance.

Even when the workpiece is entirely opaque, wait for more than 30 minutes because the center may still be liquid. When the workpiece is completely set, it can be removed from the mold.

32

Make a Silicone Protector for Soldering Irons

by **Gilson Domingues** and **Pietro Domingues**

Figure 32.1: The long metal part of a soldering iron invites burns.

Figure 32.2: Silicone protector on the soldering iron.

There are many ways to construct electronic circuits quickly and safely by using items such as breadboards, conductive inks, and kits with magnetic contacts. However, soldering is the best way to create robust circuits at a low cost.

Handling the soldering iron may offer some risks to the user, especially children. To avoid these risks, it is recommended to use personal protective equipment such as gloves and safety glasses. Even with protection, the metallic part of the soldering iron (fig. 32.1) is too long (especially for small hands) and burns are all too frequent.

Based on this, we developed a silicone protector (fig. 32.2) that is simple to make.

Instructions

1. Cut a semirigid plastic film such as obtained from folders, cards, and packages the same length as the metallic part of the soldering iron.

2. Make a tube a bit bigger than the soldering iron shaft out of the plastic film.

3. Secure the tube with adhesive tape.

4. Now make a lid for the tube. First, stand the tube on a piece of the plastic film, and draw a circle of the same diameter. Add square tabs around the circle.

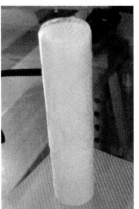 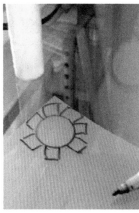

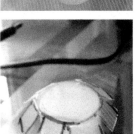

Then, cut the plastic film around the tabs.

5. Glue or tape the lid on the tube, folding the tabs down over the tube.

6. **Important:** This tube is a mold for the silicone, so if there are any gaps, the liquid silicone will leak. Wrap thin PVC film (plastic cling wrap) around the tube, so it covers any possible gaps.

7. Fix the tube rigidly at a vertical position with the lid at the bottom.

8. Prepare the silicone and pour into the tube. Fill the tube halfway to leave room for the soldering iron.

9. While the silicone is still liquid, put the cold soldering iron inside the tube, keeping it upright and in the middle.

10. When ready, pull the soldering iron out of the mold and remove the wrap.

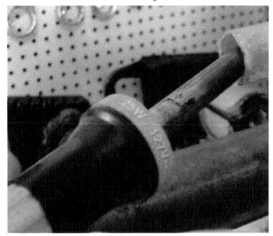

11. Place the silicone protector back on the soldering iron. Trim so that it exposes the tip of the soldering iron.

Note: The first time the protector is used, the soldering iron may smell of silicone due to the heat. Use it in a well-ventilated location. Silicone is an excellent thermal insulator, but after many minutes of use the silicone may still get warm.

Learning to Debug Circuits with CircuitScribe

by David Malpica

When we took upon the challenge of teaching basic circuitry to sixth-grade students as part of our skillbuilder activities, we used a variety of kits and tools, including paper circuits, soldering, and CircuitScribe,[1] a conductive ink kit that also has an online circuit simulator. One common pitfall when studying circuits is when students create short circuits, which leads to many problems including nonworking circuits (and frustrated students) and possibly damaged and nonreusable materials (and frustrated teachers).

When we first started using paper circuits we used templates from the *Circuit Sticker Sketchbook: LEDs, Switches & Sensors* by Jie Qi.[2] Students were extremely excited to create their first working circuit with LEDs and quickly moved on to more complex series and parallel circuits. An advantage of the template (fig. 33.1) is that it's very difficult for students to accidentally create a short circuit.

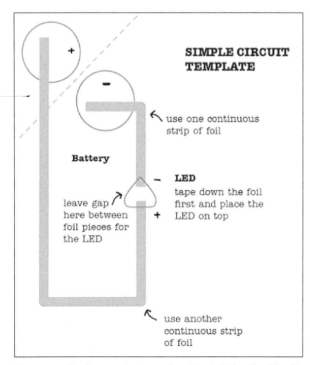

Figure 33.1: Simple paper circuit template (Circuit Sticker Sketchbook).

Figure 33.2: Soldering station.

We then taught the students to solder leads onto the paper circuits. This was also extremely engaging for students. While we ran a soldering station (fig. 33.2) with half the class, the other half was trying out the CircuitScribe kits. The free-flow nature of the conductive ink pen allowed students to create networks of ink in any shape. While the freedom felt good, this allowed students to create short circuits without knowing. The CircuitScribe modules are protected against damage and helpfully show short circuits through red LEDs.

It became clear that at least part of the underlying theory had to be explained in order to quickly have all kids be able to identify short circuits. Using CircuitScribe's online simulator, we designed four circuits, one working and three nonworking ones (figs. 33.3 and 33.4).[3] The software's editing mode has tools to help students quickly visualize the circuits created by the modules and the ink paths. Using a water flow analogy, we explained that electricity likes to travel through the path of least resistance and that it would travel that way though the ink as well, bypassing the LED module if that's the easiest.

Once students understood this, they were better equipped to design circuits on their own with LEDs, buzzers, and other components.

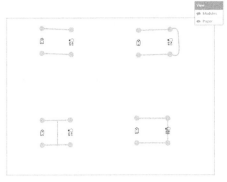

Figure 33.3: CircuitScribe's online circuit editing tool (without modules).

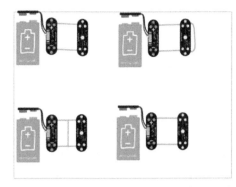

Figure 33.4: CircuitScribe's online circuit editing tool (with modules).

Notes

1. electroninks.com
2. researchideas.ca/coding/docs/Chibitronics
   _sketchbook-en-v1.pdf
3. 123d.circuits.io/circuits/808411-short-ci

Reference

Qi, J. (2014). *Circuit sticker sketchbook: LEDs, switches & sensors*. Singapore: Sutajio Ko-Usagi PTE LTD. Retrieved from researchideas.ca/coding /docs/Chibitronics_sketchbook-en-v1.pdf

Exploring Circuits: Make Stuff Light Up and Move!

by Tracy Rudzitis

Figure 34.1: Challenge accepted: an interactive toy.

My sixth- and seventh-grade STEAM students immersed themselves in the wonder of electricity based on open-ended challenges that allowed them to invent, make, and build (fig. 34.1). They started out by exploring basic circuits, using components that I constructed using the Exploratorium's electricity exploration curriculum.[1]

The overall learning targets for this unit were the following:

- To handle and connect components without overloading, damaging, or destroying them
- To learn what an electrical circuit is
- To understand and be able to measure electricity and resistance
- To draw, build, and identify the characteristics of a series circuit and a parallel circuit
- To construct a circuit of the student's own design using a variety of conductive and non-conductive materials that include a switch, an output device, and a sensor (input device)

Tinkering and exploring how circuits and electricity works generated many questions from the students. We wrote down some of the questions[2] so we could use these ideas to drive the projects that students would immerse themselves in to really develop their understanding of electricity.

My approach to student inquiry into content is that it should be directly related to questions they have about how and why things work. Without providing all the answers upfront, students will choose project ideas that might answer some of the questions they have about the subject we are in the midst of.

To challenge my students to think big about what they wanted to make, I provided some very big prompts:

- Build something that can see.
- Build something that can talk.
- Build something that makes sounds and responds to touch.
- Build something that makes art.
- Build an interactive toy.
- Build something that performs a simple task that makes life easier.
- Build something that helps people.
- Build something that you can wear.
- Build something that makes music.
- Build an interactive house.
- Build something powered by the sun.

I didn't want students to think about the tools or materials that would be used in the projects at first—I wanted them to think about ideas and what they were curious about. Once the students decided upon an idea, I was able to direct them toward the kind of materials or existing projects that they could use as resources and reference for their own work.[3] Students who were a bit overwhelmed could choose from some ideas and examples I had in the classroom: simple soft circuits or paper circuits that could be made with simple materials yet still allow for students to demonstrate their understanding of the learning targets that make up a middle school science class.

I wanted students to use a range of materials. I saw this project as having the potential to showcase the different materials and electronics that are available in the STEAM lab. I pointed students in the direction of the Arduino, MaKey MaKey, Make!Sense boards, Hummingbirds, and NXT Bricks. I provided solar panels, various DC motors and servos, LEDs and batteries, and lots of wire and copper tape. The students' imaginations and creativity filled in the gaps, and the results were pretty spectacular.

Students documented their work and wrote up instructions that we published as PDF files on our STEAM lab site[4] so that others could share in the experience of making and learning and exploring electricity. This documentation can inspire and provide some instructions and ideas so that others can make these projects. The photos and videos that students took of their work, as it was being made or as finished products, give a glimpse into the process, thinking, and questions that happen as the project unfolds.

When students are engaged and motivated by exploring their own questions, ideas, and interests, they learn so much, and better yet, really retain so much of what it is that we want them to learn. By embedding the learning in rich and sometimes difficult and complex activity, the student comes away with a deeper understanding. Sharing in these experiences and wonderfully creative ideas and inventions that only middle school students can have, the teacher comes away with new ideas, a deeper understanding, and admiration for the amazing minds of these students.

Notes

1. tinkering.exploratorium.edu/circuit-boards
2. sites.google.com/a/thecomputerschool.org /steam-cs/home-1/ questionswehaveaboutelectricity
3. Instructables is a great source for ideas: instructables.com
4. sites.google.com/a/thecomputerschool.org /steam-cs/home-1/circuitprojectdocumentation

Project Snapshots

This collection of projects contains some of the favorite projects of the FabLearn Fellows. These are go-to activities that always work, projects that were especially engaging, or tried-and-tested projects that showcase thoughtful educational practice and student-centered learning with modern materials. The projects are short and free-form, capturing the essential heart and soul of the project instead of trying to fit them into a one-size-fits-all "lesson plan" template.

These project snapshots accommodate a wide variety of grades and experience levels, vary in length and expertise needed, and use many different tools, materials, software, and hardware. This wide variation may seem random, but it is deliberate. One of the challenges of creating a coherent set of resources about making in learning spaces is that there are so many variations in tools, spaces, time, subjects, and experience levels. We have embraced the chaos with this grab bag of favorites.

These projects showcase the remarkable variety and range that happens in student-centered environments rich in materials and imagination. They are organized by the kind of learning space where the project is situated—whether a community organization, museum, or school—then by author. (See appendix for consolidated list of snapshots with grade or age level as well as tools, materials and supplies, and recommended software.)

We invite you to view these projects as starting points rather than complete recipes. Many projects have resources to learn more, and every FabLearn Fellow has a page on the FabLearn site (fablearn.stanford.edu/fellows/fellows) where he or she can be contacted. Browse and find the ones that speak to you. Many are works in progress, but that's how making works! (Iterative design isn't just for kids.)

35 Community Organizations

FabLearn Fellows who work in community organizations are both educators and leaders in their communities. Making as a practice in these learning spaces takes its place alongside youth empowerment, civic responsibility, and community improvement. They often take on added responsibilities such as teacher professional development for local schools. In contrast to schools, projects in community organizations do not have to fall into neat timelines or rigid subject areas and often include collaboration with people of all ages. They give young people opportunities to pursue activities that fall outside standard school subjects without the threat or promise of a grade at the end.

The noticeable component of these projects is youth agency. Young people (mostly) come to community centers because they want to, not because they have to. They return if they find something meaningful to return to. Community organizations must create obvious social value and offer experiences that are welcoming and inclusive of newcomers and veterans alike. The projects that follow are thoughtful examples that meet this high bar.

Susan Klimczak

Susan is the education organizer of the Learn 2 Teach, Teach 2 Learn program at South End Technology Center @ Tent City in Boston, Massachusetts, United States, which provides free or low-cost access and training in computer-related technology to the community.

Flappy Bird game making with Scratch

After the youth teachers (teens) had made their own Flappy Bird games with physics simulations for gravity, we wanted to create a much simpler version to teach younger children in two hours. To do this, we use a starter game in Scratch, with many choices for flappies, tubes, and backgrounds that children can remix.[1]

Figure 35.1: Flappy Bird Guide handout explains how to make your own Flappy Bird game.

The youth teachers created a two-page single fold guide for the children (fig. 35.1) with hints to scaffold the game building.

The youth teachers also created an explainer guide[2] and a cheat sheet[3] to help them prepare for teaching and to consult if they run into problems while teaching.

Musical Scratch

In each step of this beginning Scratch tutorial activity the children learn a new technique in Scratch while creating an interactive character.

Before the activity, decide how many parts the characters will have and what will be interactive about it. For example, characters with eight parts could have a head, upper and lower body, four arms/legs, and a tail. The interactivity options can be any Scratch techniques you want the students to learn. The game proceeds like musical chairs without taking chairs away; the children each draw part of the character and add interactivity, but when the music plays, they have to switch computers and work on another character.

The children loved moving around and dancing to the music. We used smartphones to play their favorite songs for the musical chairs part of the activity.

Wooden cell phone holders

Our youth teachers suggested that we make cell phone holders fabricated in wood and acrylic as an Introduction to Digital Design and Fabrication Project. An experienced youth teacher made a press-fit demonstration template that the new youth teachers could build upon (fig. 35.2).

Figure 35.2: Proud owners of newly fabricated wooden cell phone holders.

The project allowed the youth teachers to learn the basics of formatting bitmap drawings into vector drawings while designing with Inkscape and LibreDraw.

MaKey MaKey game controllers

We like having youth make conductive MaKey MaKey game controllers and create a way to personalize games.

One example is a Scratch rock, paper, scissors game. We found a version that featured white hands, but since most of our youth are youth of color, we substituted hands of color. We also personalized the game and created laughs by making versions with college mentors, and one featured the principal and science/math department head at a local middle school where we taught.[4]

Having the children both personalize the Scratch program and construct a game controller—using a wide variety of conductive materials from pencils to fruit—is very engaging.

Another popular example is the Whack-a-Potato game from BluntBody,[5] based on the popular whack-a-mole game. We create a pack of possible "moles" that range from popular cartoon characters (e.g., SpongeBob SquarePants, Hello Kitty) to music stars such as Beyoncé. We also use GIMP[6] (a free image editor) to take photos and encourage youth to put themselves or their friends into the Whack-a-Potato game.

MaKey MaKey conductivity game

We use MaKey MaKeys in many ways, but one of our favorite activities is having a "battery battle." Last year, a group of youth leaders from the Netherlands came to visit us and shared a Scratch program they used as a competitive game with MaKey MaKey. We break up the group of youth into two groups: Team Blau and Team Rood. We set up a table of many different kinds of things— some conductive, some not, and the sillier the better—and each team has to choose one item they think is conductive. If they are right, a battery on the screen gets a bar. The first team to get five bars wins.

We created documentation including an activity plan[7] and an edited version of the Scratch program that makes it much easier to set up.[8]

Squishy circuit activities

We have been developing activities with squishy circuit dough (homemade conductive and insulating dough) for many years.[9] These are some of the things we have done:

- Made buzzers buzz with both a battery pack and a solar panel to highlight the power of sustainable forms of energy
- Created solar spin art by making a squishy motor circuit powered by a larger solar panel, and using watered-down tempera paint
- Explored Squishy Circuit–powered RGB LEDs, which the youth at a local middle school where we piloted the activity just loved
- Created a variation on the board game Operation called Rescue Me!, which focuses on building a circuit from a diagram and has the added benefit that it is very transportable for the activities we do at community organizations all around Boston

Machines Gone Wild!:
Physical programming with cam mechanisms

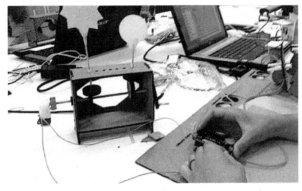

Figure 35.3: Automata with cam mechanism.

This activity helps our youth learn about mechanical engineering with mechanisms and physical programming with Arduinos (fig. 35.3). So many of our youth "think with their hands" while building and yet automata or mechanisms that would put this to good use are rarely taught in their schools.

To develop this project, we took our inspiration from the San Francisco Exploratorium Cam Mechanism project.[10]

At Learn 2 Teach, Teach 2 Learn we repeat each activity four times because our thirty-four youth teachers are divided into small learning groups of eight or nine. This works wonderfully for piloting and developing activities. Each week we get feedback from youth teachers about what would make the activity better for them and then improve our activity design for the next week. The first week, we had youth teachers cut and build the cam boxes themselves, but they suggested that we fabricate the cam boxes so that they could spend most of their time experimenting with the automata cam mechanisms rather than cutting cardboard.

This was a key factor in improving the activity and focusing on what is really important.

For this physical programming activity, we used Arduinos with a Modkit MotoProto Shield, plug-in components (LEDs, potentiometers, buttons, geared motors), and Modkit Micro as the graphical programming environment. Additional details, plans, and materials can be found on my FabLearn blog.[11]

Paper electronic storytelling
We have worked with Jie Qi at the MIT Media Lab on paper electronic storytelling. Jie's research has resulted in most of the paper circuits being used in makerspaces today. As she developed new paper circuit components in the MIT lab, we would help her figure out the best ways to teach them. Our youth love making light-up electronic greeting cards, and returning youth teachers even offered a workshop for youth teacher applicants that took the circuits 3D with electronic pop-up books and light-up origami.[12]

No-sew electric friends
We wanted to develop a soft-circuit activity for children that did not involve sewing, so we created digital fabrication files for the slot and tab design and fabricated the bodies out of felt (fig. 35.4). The circuits are fixed to the felt with masking tape. Two dangling legs or arms with sticky copper tape form the switch to turn on the light.

Figure 35.4: Everyone needs a soft-circuit friend.

After making their own soft circuit friends (fig. 35.5), the teenage youth teachers created a rough activity plan[13] and handout for younger students.[14] The PDFs for the outside and inside of the handout can be printed two-sided and folded down the middle.

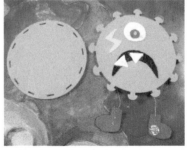
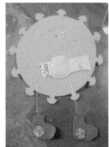

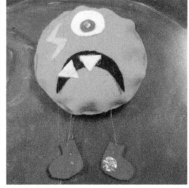

Figure 35.5: Soft-circuit electronics without sewing.

RoboPicasso: Physical programming with VEX Robotics

Figure 35.6: RoboPicasso workshop.

We have been refining a RoboPicasso physical programming activity in which youth teach a robot to draw. Before that we fabricated simple drawing robots (DrawBots) using LEGO motors.

When some VEX Robotics kits were donated, we were able to make more sophisticated Draw-Bots so that the "pen up" and "pen down" commands could be programmed and a gear train added that allowed for a much more precise design (fig. 35.6). The Modkit Micro graphical interface programming environment (developed by longtime staff and contributor Ed Baafi) lets us scaffold the learning of coding. The activity also featured a kinesthetic exercise called Moving Like a Robot and, in the end, we created a gallery of robot art (fig. 35.7).

Figure 35.7: RoboPicasso gallery.

Chain-reaction machines with WeDo and Scratch: Physical programming

Using LEGO WeDo kits, we have developed a Chain Reaction activity for our youth teachers to take to six hundred elementary and middle school youth in twenty Boston community centers for our free three-week STEAM camps.

We held a workshop at the MIT Media Lab with Abdulrahman Idlbi, a doctoral student who developed the Scratch plug in that allows the WeDo kits to connect to Scratch programs.[15] The WeDo kits have two sensors and a motor. If you use the WeDo plug-in on Scratch, you can read data from the external sensors and start the motors from Scratch. We built chain reaction machines that took motion from the physical world, through the sensors to the digital world, then back again.

Afterward, the youth teachers created a video celebration of the workshop and all the chain reaction machines.[16]

Starter project templates for Scratch game making

Youth get interested in computer programming when they have early successes with cool projects. While they love drawing in Scratch or editing imported cartoon characters, for short game-making sessions

Figure 35.8: Flappy Bird game starter Scratch project.

(as a second Scratch lesson) we use starter games with lots of sprite choices. We usually only have ninety minutes to two hours with the youth we teach in summer STEAM camp sessions, so we try to focus on students having as deep an experience as possible without us doing too much for them. It's a constant effort to balance this. One summer, we taught PAC-MAN and had a pack of different PAC-MAN figures, ghosts, and coins that the youth could use to design their games.[17] In a similar way, we have also used Flappy Bird (see page 106) with a starter kit of birds and tubes to get them started (fig. 35.8).[18]

Soft circuit pins and wearables

Figure 35.9: Soft-circuit pins are a favorite activity.

One of our tried-and-true activities to introduce both youth and adults to soft-circuit electronics is to sew circuits into wearable pins, cell phone holders, bracelets, or other small objects. In some workshops, we design and fabricate template pieces in felt on our laser cutters. In others the participants decide what to make and cut the felt themselves. It takes about four hours (fig. 35.9).

For this project we fabricate and sew battery holders for the participants to get started. I have a small felt panel that shows the stages of building the circuit and attaching the battery holder, which has been much more helpful than written documents. They can actually see what the circuit looks like. We use regular LEDs and tiny pieces of copper tape as well as conductive thread, which makes it affordable. It's important to have lots of craft materials for embellishing. This is an excellent activity for family workshops (fig. 35.10).

Figure 35.10: Family soft-circuit workshop.

Notes

1. scratch.mit.edu/projects/22357673
2. Flappy Bird Guide:
   fablearn.stanford.edu/fellows /MeaningfulMaking/FlappyBirdGuide.pdf
   Flappy Explainer Guide:
   fablearn.stanford.edu/fellows /MeaningfulMaking/FlappyExplainerGuide.pdf
3. Get Flappy Cheat Sheet:
   fablearn.stanford.edu/fellows /MeaningfulMaking/GetFlappyCheatSheet.pdf
4. College mentor Xia:
   scratch.mit.edu/projects/23582670
   Ms. Davis, math/science coordinator:
   scratch.mit.edu/projects/23581911
   Principal Brewer:
   scratch.mit.edu/projects/23578541
5. bluntbody.com/whack-a-potato
6. gimp.org
7. fablearn.stanford.edu/fellows /MeaningfulMaking /MaKeyMaKeyConductivityActivity.pdf
8. scratch.mit.edu/projects/11712714
9. fablearn.stanford.edu/fellows/blog /rethinking-squishy-circuits
10. tinkering.exploratorium.edu /cardboard-automata
11. fablearn.stanford.edu/fellows/blog /machines-gone-wild-physical -programming-cam-driven-mechanisms
12. First paper electronic storytelling workshop:
    youtu.be/c6R8ixuVBVE
    Subsequent paper electronic workshop built by youth teachers:
    flickr.com/photos/28629285@N02 /sets/72157643153856833
    Circuit sticker storytelling workshop:
    youtu.be/MQtPhaVraZA
13. fablearn.stanford.edu/fellows /MeaningfulMaking /ElectricFriendsActivityPlan.pdf
14. fablearn.stanford.edu/fellows /MeaningfulMaking /ElectricFriendCheatSheet.pdf
15. wiki.scratch.mit.edu/wiki/LEGO _Education_WeDo_Robotics_Kit
16. youtu.be/l6gYRjOCIoc
17. scratch.mit.edu/projects/11132470
18. scratch.mit.edu/projects/22357673

Susanna Tesconi

Susanna is a learning environments designer and researcher at LABoral Centro de Arte y Creación Industrial, in Asturias, Spain, a center for research on the creative applications of digital manufacturing, offering cultural programs, workshops, and activities that foster the cultural and economic development of the community.

Hidden sound: Experimenting with piezos, vibration, and amplifiers

Figure 35.11: Sound generator with a speaker.

This is one-day workshop introduction to sound and vibration. Participants create a circuit with a 9-volt battery, one piezo buzzer, a mini–jack connector, a speaker, an amplifier, and a piece of wood (fig. 35.11).[1] (A simpler version with just the piezo and the connector requires an external amplifier.) The piezo placed on the wood (or other material) allows you to "hear" the hidden sound produced by the vibration of material. The complex version is a stand-alone sound machine; the simple version needs to be plugged into an external device to hear it.

The kids enjoy making noise, noisy storytelling, and decorating their sound machines. If you have a multichannel DJ mixer, you can plug in several instruments and set up a noisy orchestra. The kids love to bring the instruments home and make experimental electronic music.

Playing with light: Lamp design

This school-year-long project was first completed by a small group of high school students in a special program to prevent school dropouts. We asked them to research light, its everyday use, and its application to opaque projectors and other similar devices. Then we focused on lamp design and production. They worked with Inkscape and laser cutting to make prototypes using different materials and techniques (fig. 35.12) and experimented with LEDs, colors, and circuits.

Figure 35.12: Laser-cut lamp designs.

Candy monsters

In this weekend project for primary school kids, we created candy molds from 3D models using a milling machine (figs. 35.13 and 35.14). (A 3D

Figure 35.13: Milled candy molds.

printer works as well.) These photos were taken in 2009 so the modeling was done in Rhino software (fig. 35.15), an early 3D CAD software tool, which

required adult intervention in order to allow a full progression starting from freehand drawing to extrusion. Today, Tinkercad is recommended.

Figure 35.14: Homemade candy.

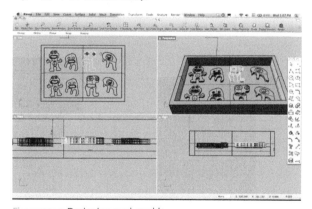

Figure 35.15: Designing candy molds.

Light gloves and light fingers

This is a scalable e-textile project. The idea is to build wearable devices for light painting, long-exposure photos that show light traces. Depending on the age and expertise of the group, different designs for the circuit and the object can be used. A good place to start is a simple "finger" made with foam, copper tape, and a single LED (no sewing). A more complex device is shown in figure 35.16, with three LEDs on a glove with an embedded sewed circuit.[2] Both simple and complex devices work well for light painting.

Figure 35.16: Light gloves for light painting.

Teacher training: No-battery lab

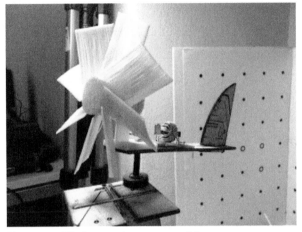

Figure 35.17: Wind-powered generator model.

In this week-long workshop, middle school teachers designed and built devices producing energy without a battery. They made wind and water-powered generator models optimized with a Joule Thief voltage booster circuit (figs. 35.17 and 35.18).

Figure 35.18: Water-powered generator model.

Teacher training: Montessori-inspired material

This is a one-week workshop for primary school teachers. After running a set of introductory ac-

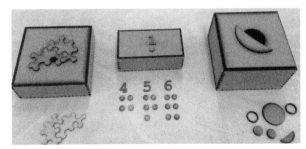

Figure 35.19: Teacher-designed and fabricated hands-on learning materials.

tivities to the Fab Lab, they used the equipment in the lab to produce materials inspired by Montessori-type instruction that they could use in the classroom (fig. 35.19).

Make it big: Scaled-up Scrabble-type game

This is a semester-long project for high school students in a special program to prevent school dropouts. The project is the design and fabrication of an oversized Scrabble-type game. Students were asked to research the game and find technical solutions to build a 5:1 scale prototype they can use at school (fig. 35.20).

Figure 35.20: Scaling up a Scrabble-type game.

What do elderly people need?

This school-year-long project was first completed by a small group of high school students in a dropout-prevention program. We asked them to design something that could help senior citizens in their everyday life. They first researched the needs of elderly people and then designed and fabricated several prototypes of a shoehorn that also picks up shoes (fig. 35.21).

Figure 35.21: Student-designed and fabricated dual-purpose shoehorn and reaching aid.

Notes

1. Hidden sounds workshop: vimeo.com /13122229
2. Light gloves: youtu.be/u6ohyXgB8Dc

Nalin Tutiyaphuengprasert

Nalin is the lab coordinator at the Darunsikkhlai School for Innovative Learning in Bangkok, Thailand, part of the FabLearn Labs network. The school offers teacher professional development, parent outreach, along with classes for students in local K–12 schools.

Darunsikkhalai School for Innovative Learning (DSIL) established a Fab Lab with the support of Stanford's Tranformative Learning Technologies Laboratory in 2013. This Fab Lab is part of the FabLearn Labs network (formerly known as FabLab@School). DSIL, an educational initiative since 2001, aims to provide a learning laboratory that exposes educators in Thailand to project-based learning and innovative learning tools and ideas. We hope that this small school project will inspire and provoke thoughts and efforts to develop more meaningful learning experiences for Thai students.

As a constructionist school since 2001, DSIL has experience in making for learning in the classroom by using paper and craft materials. Introducing digital fabrication to Thailand is another big step to make learning (especially in math and science) more concrete and interesting to students.

After some basic training for teachers and lab staff, our team of freelance designer (Sangaroon Jiamsawadi), freelance programmer (Meechai Junpho), and me as a teacher has been developing curricula and activities from scratch. We are interested in developing a curriculum and program that allows K–12 students access to a variety of fabrication tools with the aim of developing student agency and ownership of their own learning.

The activities below include those that we had developed and applied in our Fab Lab class and those that we use with teachers and parents to help them understand the new learning environment that the children will be exposed to. Developing common understanding and belief in both teachers and parents can enhance children's learning experiences and become a sustained learning environment in the long term.

Parents' maker day

The objective is to give parents the direct experience of making something in the Fab Lab. This is a good strategy to introduce the Fab Lab to parents, so they get to see it, use the devices, and ask questions.

Figure 35.22: Parents design lamps.

The activity is to make a lamp that parents can take home. The parents use Adobe Illustrator and the laser cutter, and assemble all pieces together (figs. 35.22 and 25.23).[1] At the end we have a reflection discussion with parents, introducing them to the concepts of *constructivist* and *constructionist* learning in making experiences.

Figure 35.23: Finished laser-cut lamps.

Videoconference to showcase students' ideas

Although we have tried to connect to schools outside of Thailand so kids can share their projects, the time difference has been a challenge. We

Figure 35.24: Students show their projects to visitors from across the globe.

have done a sharing session with Paulo Blikstein and Roger Sipitakiat (a lecturer from Chiangmai University) so the students could share their individual projects and get feedback from people outside the school. The students were so excited and proud of their work (fig. 35.24).

This activity can motivate the students to spend the time to improve their work. We're always looking for a school to do a videoconference with us. The kids are ready to stay overnight at school to be able to have a videoconference with a school on the other side of the world.

Fab Lab in your class (for teachers)

The objective is to think of how to promote making for teachers in regular classrooms. The Fab Lab team invited different groups of teachers to meetings and provided ideas of cool things we can make for each subject area. The Fab Lab team also worked together with the teachers running the class, not just providing ideas.

This strategy worked well, resulting in more classes involved with making in the classroom and students making in both regular class projects and the Fab Lab classes.

Minisculpture (first-time makers, ages 5–7)

Figure 35.25: Making sculptures brings ideas to life.

When the younger kids came up with brilliant ideas that they couldn't make by themselves, we designed activities to help them practice and strengthen their hand muscles while exposing them to the basic forming and structure of the object. We provided clay, wire, and construction paper, showed them how to form the shape from each material, and let them design and make their own sculptures (fig. 35.25).

Box maker (first-time makers, ages 6–8)

We created this activity for new makers, so they could enjoy the making experience instead of getting overwhelmed by the lab and experienced makers. The objective is to make a box that will not fall apart. We provided cube box plates, which

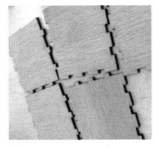

Figure 35.26: Box templates. Figure 35.27: Completed boxes.

we made by using the MakerCase website, which creates customizable laser-cut design templates.[2] We asked the kids to assemble them, glue them, and make them as strong as possible. Afterwards we test them by throwing them up in the air so they drop on the floor and hopefully do not break (figs. 35.26 and 35.27).

Design your house (beginner makers, ages 7–8)

Figure 35.28: Beginner makers design houses.

After the children made boxes in the box-maker project, we gave them a more complicated task: making a house. We created the template, taught them how to use basic tools in Adobe Illustrator, and had them design the house. They were guided through the process of designing, laser cutting, and assembly. Kids become more confident to make and use the equipment in the lab during this activity (fig. 35.28).

Pop-pop boat competition (ages 8–11)

The Fab Lab can be overwhelming to new makers, so we designed a pop-pop boat competition for starter classes to introduce them to the making experience. Pop-pop boats are made from recycled trash such as a can, milk carton, or straws. The boats are powered by heating a bit of water with a candle that escapes through the straws,[3] making a popping sound.

This project takes three one-hour classes.

- **Class 1:** The objective is to introduce the pop-pop boat. Kids work in groups of three to make their first pop-pop boat with the recycled materials.
- **Class 2:** The objective is to revise the boat designs to make the fastest boat. In groups of

two, they make a new version of the boat. They can think of other materials and designs to make it faster. They learn new techniques from each other.

- **Class 3:** They finish the boats and we have the competition. Afterward we discuss what makes the boats go fast.

Elevation drawing (ages 9–12)

This project was introduced to students after they had made a couple of things in the Fab Lab so they would already be familiar with the equipment and basic tools. With this project, kids see the benefit of spending time and effort on drawing (fig. 35.29).

Figure 35.29: Elevation drawing project.

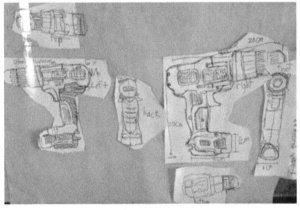
Figure 35.30: Six perspectives to see the whole.

The objective is to introduce students to the six perspectives of drawing from different points of view: top, bottom, left, right, front, and back (fig. 35.30). Students become familiar with dimensions of the object (fig. 35.31), which is helpful for the first-timer getting into 3D graphic design on the computer.

The students spend about 30 to 40 minutes drawing an object in different perspectives. The class is simple and straightforward, but the students become focused on the task (fig. 35.32). Some want to be professional designers and know that this will help them

Figure 35.31: Measuring precisely is worth the time.

Figure 35.32: Drawing can be engaging and is a skill children value.

communicate their ideas to others. They learn to use the Vernier caliper and improve their accuracy and precision. This activity familiarizes kids with millimeter units and slows them down a lot, preventing mistakes. This also helps improve the focus and concentration for many active students.

Mother's Day pop-up card with basic electronic circuits (ages 6–8)

We have students make pop-up cards for their mothers on Mother's Day (August 12 in Thailand). While making them, the students learn about basic circuits using batteries, a switch, and LEDs (fig. 35.33). There are three different classes of forty-five minutes.

Figure 35.33: Making electronic pop-up cards for Mother's Day.

- **Class 1:** Make the basic pop-up card (as an individual task).
- **Class 2:** Make circuits work. Connect the battery, wires, and switch to make the LED light up (in groups of two).
- **Class 3:** Combine all tasks, making pop-up cards with one LED in their own design.

Notes

1. Author's blog: dsilfablabatschool.wordpress.com/events-and-workshops/parents-maker-workshop
2. makercase.com
3. Video showing how to make pop-pop boats: youtu.be/0ki9Kta8g14
   Note: The gluing step is not as easy as it looks in the video. We did some trials by our team first.

Juliet Wanyiri

Juliet is the founder of Foondi Workshops in Nairobi, Kenya, which runs collaborative design workshops for children and adults with the aim of capacity building and skill sharing.

Redesigning our cities

Figure 35.34: Designing the city of the future.

We asked kids to design a futuristic Nairobi, Kenya. This three-month project was spread out so the children were able to build projects on architecture and design as well as tinker with electronics in transport, security, and *funtomatics* (a word we coined to mean "fun electronic projects and games"). It engages students in physical programming, 3D printing, laser cutting, and e-textiles (fig. 35.34). Want to know what the future will look like? Ask your students to show you!

Video games and virtual worlds: Programming with Scratch

Introduce software programming and gaming by having kids experiment building their own virtual world, and building games around themes that engage them in a fun and creative way.[1]

Intelligent house and car

To get kids to dive into an electronics kit, ask them to imagine their dream house or car and let them make it. It gives them a great chance to use sensors, lights, motors, and LEGO bricks to reimagine the world around them and see themselves as positive change makers.

Building a bike-powered smoothie maker (bici-blender)

What's the one type of transport you can find in any part of the world? A bike? That's right. Now Foondi Workshops is rethinking how we can use bicycles in emerging markets where access to reliable and affordable energy remains out of reach for thousands of people. Foondi held a hands-on design workshop on building a bici-blender (fig. 35.35). This project is ideal for older kids to learn about mechanics and

Figure 35.35: Fitting the blender to the bicycle.

how to use pedal-powered machinery.[2] There are several adaptations[3] of this, each made to suit the materials available and the user needs.

3D printing meets paper electronics

Looking for a way to introduce six-year-olds to 3D printing? Have them 3D print their names and their favorite superhero logo. Then make a paper circuit, an LED, and a coin battery, and voila! You have a cool electronic name tag for your kids to wear during the maker sessions.

The clapping car: An introduction to sensors

Figure 35.36: The clapping car.

Using the sound sensor, motor, and LEGO pieces in the PicoCricket kit,[4] the students are able to build a sound-controlled car that begins to move when they clap (or any other loud sound is made) and moves in the opposite direction when they clap again (fig. 35.36). This project introduces the concept of sensor control incorporated into the normal functionality of a simple car.

From here, the students are able to build even more creative, intelligent electronics projects on home automation, security, and automated games.

Electronic quiz board

Students loved an electronic quiz game we made using the PicoCricket, so we had them make their own quiz boards (fig. 35.37). The PicoCricket was no longer available and electronic kits are hard to ship to Kenya, so they had to

Figure 35.37: Electronic quiz boards.

make their own designs. The students link each word with the correct answer. If a correct match is made, the light goes on. If not, they need to try again until they get it right. These are the materials we used:

- A bulb and bulb holder
- One 9-volt battery
- Screws (for each question and its corresponding answer)
- Alligator clips
- Cardboard to act as the quiz board

The kids enjoyed building these boards and testing their knowledge on everything from the animal kingdom to countries and their respective capital cities. Using the quiz board, they were able to create their own learning environment based on the electronics and prior maker classes.

Simple origami lights

This project incorporates science in art by building functional art. It's very easy to make.

Figure 35.38: Origami lights.

Here's what you need:

- Paper to build the origami
- One LED
- Coin cell battery
- Wires

Tape the LED to the coin cell battery so the light comes on. Fold the origami around the LED and battery. The origami will glow for days.

This project teaches kids how LEDs work and the basics of a simple circuit design while making something beautiful (fig. 35.38).

Notes

1. Scratch tutorials and sample games: teach-ict.com/programming/scratch /scratch_home.htm
2. foondiworkshops.tumblr.com /post/89782332880/building-a-bici-blender
3. instructables.com/id/Pedal-powered -smoothie-maker
4. picocricket.com

Museums

Many museums are incorporating makerspaces and classes in making into their existing spaces and activity offerings. Museums have always offered chances to explore cool phenomena and learn at one's own pace. Discovery centers have always been makerspaces; now they can offer even more opportunities to invent and design with modern materials and electronics.

Museums have some similarity to community organizations and may serve the community in very similar ways. Thus, their maker programs are similar. They have the luxury of being able to create both short and longer sessions, and do not have to give grades. Often these projects are adaptable for a wide range of ages and can include all family members joining in.

Keith Ostfeld

Keith is the director of Educational Technology and Exhibit Development at the Children's Museum of Houston in Houston, Texas, United States, working on STEAM-related exhibit development, mobile tech/ blended learning, and making/tinkering projects for children and their families.

Cardboard automata

This is one of the first activities from the Playful Invention and Exploration Network of the San Francisco Exploratorium[1] that we implemented in our own makerspace. Cardboard automata combine simple machines with art to create whimsical moving sculptures that both children and adults love. We've hosted multiple variations of this workshop in the museum, in outreach work, and at the Houston Maker Faire.

Light painting

This activity from the Exploratorium's Playful Invention and Exploration Network[2] requires an investment in a good camera. We had the kids either make their own LED devices or use one of the light sources we provided.

Zoetrope

In this animation activity, kids first make a zoetrope that works using our premade strip; then we encourage them to try to create their own strip to animate.[3]

Duct tape making

We do lots of making with duct tape. A wallet is one of our go-to items,[4] but we also have made belts, superhero masks, and bags/purses.[5]

Top making

We've had lots of variations of tops, and they have reached a point where this has become an engineering sort of activity. We provide lots of materials as well as circle templates and safety compasses. One of my favorites is the chop top.[6]

LED bling

In a very open-ended LED jewelry-type activity, kids make rings, bracelets, glasses, and more. We usually start off with several examples around the room as inspiration and encourage the families to create their own design.

Notes

1. exploratorium.edu/pie/downloads /Cardboard_Automata.pdf
2. exploratorium.edu/pie/library /lightpainting.html
3. instructables.com/id/Make-a-Zoetrope-21
4. instructables.com/id/Duct-Tape-Wallet-14
5. instructables.com/id /Duct-Tape-Bag-okayPurse
6. instructables.com/id/Chop-Top

37

Schools

The majority of the FabLearn Fellows work in schools, however, that's where the similarity ends. These schools span a wide range of public, independent, and charter schools that include various grade levels. Some are single gender. Some are very progressive while others are more traditional. They are urban, suburban, and rural and span the globe.

In these schools, maker programs are often integrated into the school day. This offers benefits in that students come for a set period of time, often every day. Being able to count on this time means that the projects can be longer and more substantial than in drop-in or informal settings. However, a downside may be that there are many more students to accommodate, with larger classes and multiple sections. Additionally, assessment may be a greater concern, and alignment to standards such as Common Core may be required. The project snapshots below offer different ways that these schools address these concerns and adapt to their various contexts.

Schools that offer maker experiences in after-school or lunch hours may find that their projects look more like the projects from museums or community organizations. No matter what, there are a wide spectrum of tried-and-true projects and activities for you to make your own.

Jaymes Dec

Jaymes is the Fab Lab coordinator at The Marymount School of New York in New York City, New York, United States, and teaches grade 6–8 technology classes. Marymount is an independent K–12 school for girls.

Make something that makes art

This is an example of an open-ended challenge that worked well during the second semester after students had learned how to use most of the tools in the lab. It's pretty self-explanatory. I like to give kids access to tools along with vague challenges that put some constraints around the ideation process.

Interactive dioramas

Students build interactive data visualizations or museum-type diorama displays that address a biodiversity issue. They start the project by visiting a local natural history museum to observe different types of museum displays. Then they choose an issue (e.g., deforestation, pollution, invasive species) that they want to highlight. They design an interactive display that addresses that issue, using tools and materials like the 3D printers, laser cutter, vinyl cutter, Arduino, Scratch, and MaKey MaKeys.[1]

Nerdy Derby

This is an annual week-long collaboration among science, art, and technology classes. Students spend half the week doing experiments that allow them to discover some of the variables that affect the speed of a vehicle on a track. They spend the rest of the week designing and building cars to compete in a derby competition[2] for fastest car, slowest car, and Queen of the Hill.

High-contrast portraiture

Many students enjoy portraiture projects. I ask students to take a high-contrast photo of their head and manipulate it on a computer so that they can use the image to make vinyl portraits or laser-cut stencils.

MaKey MaKey instrument

Many students enjoy the "low floor" and "wide walls" of the MaKey MaKey microcontroller. One popular project is to make a novel music instrument using the MaKey MaKey and a computer. One team of students built a piano out of marshmallows and brownies. When they realized that they would run out of inputs on their controller, they learned how to reprogram and change the keys on the MaKey MaKey.

Light-up bracelet

Many students enjoy making simple felt bracelets with an LED, a battery, and snaps for a switch. This is based on The Sparkling Bracelet project in the book *Sew Electric*.[3]

Make your space a better place

This is a semester-long project where students start with a public space in the school building and come up with an interactive installation that changes how people behave in that space. Resulting projects have included light-up signs that encourage hand washing in the bathroom, a staircase that plays music, a motion-activated device that plays music in the elevator, and an RFID card reader that dishes out compliments.

Environmental concern (high school)

GreenFab was a Fab Lab program funded by the National Science Foundation for high school students from Hunts Point, South Bronx, New York. Students attended morning classes on digital design, fabrication, computer programming, and physical computing—all explored through the lens of sustainable design and green technologies. During the afternoon, students had an opportunity to tinker and explore with technologies, host visitors from environmental organizations, and go on field trips to local eco-friendly manufacturers and museums. For six weeks each semester, students worked on their own projects. The prompt that we gave them was to make something that addressed an environmental concern in their community.

We left it up to the students to come up with their own definitions of environment, concern, and community, and the students came up with great ideas. They made many impressive projects including a machine for drying nail polish, an aquaponics window farming setup, a data-collecting setup to test the effectiveness of green roofs in the summer, a mold for casting bricks from dirt and grass, and a solar-paneled park table that charged USB devices.[4]

Project ideas from Constructing Modern Knowledge 2014

Figure 37.1: CMK 2014 participants making shoes that play music when dancing.

The following is a list of ideas that teachers had for projects at the beginning of CMK 2014, a summer institute for educators.[5] Some of the ideas won't make sense out of context, but they might trigger an idea. Not all of them were built, but many were, such as the musical dance shoes shown in figure 37.1.[6]

Musical dance shoes

Wearable mouse

Motion sensor camera for race cars

Smartphone zip-line (building to building)

Wearable speakers

Flocking and/or swarm robots

Giant cardboard robot

Critter detector

Animatronic crochet

Giant drawing robot

Drones

Helio tracker

Interactive coffeepot

Conductable fountain (Bellagio)

Exercise reminder "Get Up + Move"

Magnets

Fly-on-the-wall shirt (kid follower)

Tesla (mini) coil

Choose your own adventure

Rube Goldberg machine

Automated chicken coop

Virtual orchestra conductor

Talking and self-watering plant

Phone tracker

Remote sprinkler system

Interactive wallet

Smart compost bin

Interactive recycling bin

Perpetual-motion machine

Visual voice meter

Voice pitch-meter device

Sand sculpture

Interactive soft book

Jewelry

Jumping bot

Airplay receiver

Paper speakers

Robotic creatures

Wearable greenhouse

Interactive art installation

Stress reducer/tester

Robot class pet

Gloves that translate Morse code to sign language

Program to generate stories

Weather data art generator

Animatronic parrot

Robot head massager

Wearable space invaders

Twitter (stats) meter

T-shirt that plays music

Interactive sound sculpture

Musical instruments

Stroboscope

Interactive tree sculpture

Robot high-five machine

Notes

1. marymountnyc.org/page/News-Detail ---New?pk=721062&fromId=171907
2. nerdyderby.com
3. sewelectric.org/diy-projects /sparkling-bracelet
4. Slideshow of GreenFab projects: nsf.gov/news/newsmedia/greenfab
5. constructingmodernknowledge.com Special thanks to Brian Smith for collecting this list.
6. Videos of CMK 2014 projects: vimeo.com/tag:CMK14

Gilson Domingues

Gilson is a university professor at School of Design and Architecture at Anhembi Morumbi University, in São Paulo, Brazil, where he teaches interaction design and physical computing. He also collaborates with local schools to create integrated engineering/design projects for students from the university, high school and middle school.

Assisting Gilson with these projects was Pietro Domingues, a mechatronics student at the University of São Paulo, currently working on projects related to rapid prototyping on engineering and design on engineering. He is a member of Programa de Educação Tutorial—Automação e Sistemas, where he develops projects relating to education, research, and extension inside the mechatronics undergraduate course.

Little Thomas Edisons:
Assembling and inventing (grade 6 to high school)

Figure 37.2: Monjolo mechanism.

The students learn how to build little mechanisms and how to automate them with GoGo Board[1] and Arduino. They also learn how to make basic electronic circuits and printed circuit boards (PCBs) and how to adapt other existing designs. In these activities they learn basic concepts about electromagnetism, electricity, and electronics (transistors, capacitors, resistors, relays, etc.).

The mechanism and circuit building allow the students to understand and experience the electronics and mechanics principles, but they can be understood with metaphors as well. For example, to explain the concept of oscillators we show a "Monjolo" mechanism,[2] which is a water-powered mechanical oscillator (fig. 37.2).

To build understanding, we lead students through a number of activities that isolate each concept including the following:

- Manipulating circuits using a 555 chip, changing resistor and capacitor values to obtain changes in oscillation (fig. 37.3)

- Building an LED flasher and electrical bell with relay[3]

Figure 37.3: Oscillator circuit with 555 chip.

After these more fundamental experiences, the students are able to assemble more complex circuits and combine circuits with mechanisms. They assembled their own GoGo board at Colégio Santo Américo and Fundação Pedreira (fig. 37.4).

To make the assembly task less complicated, we developed a simpler version of the GoGo board, called the GoGo Mini.[4] Eighth graders assembled this version over one semester.

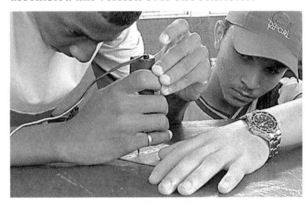

Figure 37.4: Assembling GoGo board.

Little Turings:
Programming robots and other devices

With the Gogo Board, Gogo Mini, and Arduino, students can build their own devices and robots. When the students learn basic notions about programming, their understanding about mechatronics is better.

To learn programming, the students are challenged to program little robots to execute tasks like walking until some objective is met, or to follow a black line on the floor. This helps them understand sensor reading, conditionals, and computer programming workflow in general.

Figure 37.5: *Robô barato.*

Robots worked so well that we developed a lot of versions using the Gogo board.[5] These versions interested many students and teachers, so the *Robô barato* (cheap robot) project (fig. 37.5) was successfully launched on Catarse (a crowdfunding platform in Brazil).[6]

Later we developed a cheaper and simpler model that can be made in a laser cutter and assembled by school students.[7] We tested this robot with the same eighth graders at the Alef school. This robot model allowed the students to program their own robot and learn the principles of programming.

Notes

1. gogoboard.org
2. Monjolo video: youtu.be/oGLaTd264Dw
3. fablearn.stanford.edu/fellows/project /led-flasher-and-electric-bell-relay
4. fablearn.stanford.edu/fellows/project /gogo-mini
5. luthieriaderobos.blogspot.com.br
6. catarse.me/robobarato
7. fablearn.stanford.edu/fellows/project /low-cost-robot

David Malpica

David is director of the FabLab@BCS embedded in the Bullis Charter School in Los Altos, California, United States, focusing on grades 5–8.

Engineering design intersession (grade 7)

Challenge descriptions were written by colleague Sarah Watanabe.

In between trimesters, seventh-grade students get three weeks of focused project-based engineering design. Students pick from a pool of challenges gathered by the teachers from our local school community. Below are two examples from our pool of challenges.

Stop the crows!

Figure 37.6: Stop the crows!

PROBLEM: The crows on the campus are food ninjas! They easily get into the trash cans and lunch boxes, removing food and packaging (fig. 37.6) and making a mess of our beautiful school.

YOUR JOB: STOP THOSE CROWS! Figure out a way to prevent the crows from making a mess. Make sure to interview people to determine their biggest crow concern, and then get to work preventing our bird burglars from striking again.

A heart-wrenching situation

Figure 37.7: Wrench holder.

PROBLEM: In the FabLab@BCS, twenty-two wrenches need to be stored on the pegboard and easily transported. However, the wrench holder was made of cheap plastic and broke (fig. 37.7).

YOUR JOB: Create a sturdy wrench holder that can be hung on the pegboard and easily and safely moved from place to place with the wrenches still on it.

Design the School of the Future competition (grade 8)

As one of the eighth-grade intersessions, students are tasked to submit models for the Design the School of the Future competition, called SchoolsNEXT,[1] organized by the Association for Learning Environments (formerly CEFPI). Students carefully balance pedagogical models, environmental factors, and architectural design based on a real plot of land (the school campus, fig. 37.8). In June 2015, a team of Bullis Charter School eighth graders reached the final stages of the competition.

Figure 37.10: Laser-cut animals.

a protected mythological creature. The habitat is designed in the homeroom classroom using low-cost prototyping materials.

Figure 37.8: School of the Future design.

Redesign of 3D-printed Robohands (grade 5)

As part of a unit on learning about the human body, students were given the 3D-printed components of the Snap-Together Robohand (fig. 37.9).[2] They were given the tinkering challenge of putting the parts together and observing problems with the result. They were then introduced to the use of digital calipers (be careful—these are sharp!) to take measurements and use those to rebuild 3D models of components of the hands. Finally we went through a design-thinking exercise, where they thought of improvements for the robohand (with a user in mind), and modeled those in Tinkercad.

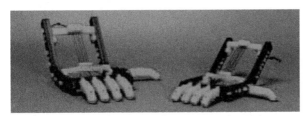

Figure 37.9: Snap-Together Robohand. *Photo courtesy of MakerBot.*

Laser-cut habitat animals and mythological creatures (grade 4)

Part of a larger project-based-learning unit, students learn how to take Omni-Animal templates[3] to create fantastic and real-world beasts and animals. Students learn to precisely design parts to fit the template (fig. 37.10). The unit is about designing a zoo habitat that would house

3D gnomes skill builder (grade 3)

When doing this project for the first time, we didn't have good Internet access, so I relied on Autodesk 123D Design instead of Tinkercad. Because it's less intuitive, teaching 123D Design to third graders

Figure 37.11: 3D gnome design.

was a challenge. However, the students showed incredible resilience in the face of crashes and not-so-intuitive tools in building gnomes (fig.

37.11). Those who finished early went on to create a musical instrument for the gnome (fig. 37.12). Overall, the results were pretty impressive.

Figure 37.12: Gnome with musical instrument.

This skill builder was a preamble for a more in-depth project-based learning unit where students had to redesign inventions in history (such as wind turbines, telephones, and cars). I showed the students different CAD tools (such as extrusion, revolve, sweep, mirror, loft) and had them look for or think of real-world industrial designs that use those techniques.

Since the gnomes were practice projects, they weren't 3D printed. Furthermore, many of these had unattached components, and they would have come apart if printed. That was a concept that had to be constantly revisited: some things that look like good 3D designs can't be made in the real world.

Kinetic sculptures (grade 8 STEAM unit)

In collaboration with the art teacher, eighth-grade students designed kinetic art sculptures in the FabLab@BCS. Kinetic sculptures are a perfect way

Figure 37.13: Kinetic sculpture.

for students to be engaged in STEAM integration (fig. 37.13). The students' work was inspired by artists and designers such as U-ram Choe, Doris Sung, Theo Jansen, Reuben Margolin, and Alexander Calder.

Turtle racing game (grade 6 engineering design)

Students are introduced to design and programming through a series of TurtleArt or Pencil-Code coding exercises. The students use their graphics as part of a larger Scratch project

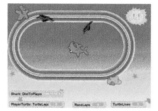

Figure 37.14: Student-designed game.

in which they are challenged to create a game where sea turtles race against each other through sand and water and avoid opponents such as sharks and crabs (fig. 37.14).

Costa Rica eco-tourism experience (grade 6)

After visiting a sea-turtle research and protection station in Costa Rica, students were tasked to design an eco-tourism experience that will protect the environment and its inhabitants, and help the economy of nearby town Tamarindo. In the lab students used software such as

Figure 37.15: Eco-friendly structure design.

123D Design and 123D Make to design cardboard structures representing their eco-tourism experiences (fig. 37.15).

Notes

1. cefpi.org/websites/main/index.php?p=161
2. thingiverse.com/thing:92937
3. tltl.stanford.edu/project/omni-animal

Heather Allen Pang

Heather is a history teacher at Castilleja School in Palo Alto, California, United States, an independent school for girls in grades 6–12.

National History Day exhibit boards

This is not really a maker project but rather an extension of a more traditional project that has greatly improved since we started making. Students do an extensive research project related to the National History Day theme. They have several options of how to present their research, including making a museum-style exhibit. Students at first think this is a traditional poster board, and then they look at some of the projects from previous years and realize what a building project it is.

Advisory project modified for laser cutter

Students have a conversation in their advisory class about what matters to them and how they might want to remember things they want to accomplish during the day, week, or school year. Students come up with words to stand for their goals, like *friendship*, *courage*, and *creativity*, and then they make a necklace, bracelet, or backpack decoration with one of the words.

Although I have been limited to the words on charms I can find at the local craft store, I am going to do the exercise to create the word list, and then take the students down to the laser cutter (or if the timing doesn't work, I will cut the words on the laser cutter), so they can have any word they want on their "word reminder."

Lined bag: Introduction to sewing by machine

Figure 37.16: Sewing machine practice. Figure 37.17: Hand-cut pattern.

This is the first project in a nine-period sewing elective. It is challenging but doable for students who have limited sewing experience. It is also useful for showing how 3D objects are made from flat cloth.

Students create their own patterns. (If you are short on time, you can make the patterns for them.) The bags are lined, so they need four cut

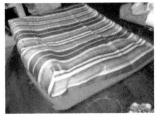

Figure 37.18: Completed bag.

pieces of the pattern, and then we talk our way through sewing each step (figs. 37.16–18), leaving a bit open to turn the bag. Students may add an optional strap. We use recycled fabric from a local shop.

Skill builder: Inkscape buildings (grade 8)

The students in the monument project (see chapter 26) said one of the biggest challenges was getting their ideas drawn in Inkscape to cut out on the laser cutter, so I set up a skill-builder project to familiarize them with the program earlier in the year.

I assigned each student an American skyscraper or tall building, ranging in height from 300 to over 14,000 feet, and gave them each an image of the building. They had to import the image and trace the shapes. I reminded them that breaking something down into shapes was a seventh-grade math skill, so that was a good review. The students had very detailed instructions. (I learned early on that to get students to follow the instructions, I would not answer questions that did not start with what step they were on, which cut down on the questions considerably.)

Figure 37.19: Skyscrapers.

After I displayed the buildings in the classroom (fig. 37.19), we had a great conversation about how the skyscraper changed cities, the technology needed to build them, and the problems of urbanization.

Figure 37.20: Laser-cut Williamsburg. We are still working on some issues of scale.

We have also done this project with eighteenth-century buildings from Colonial Williamsburg and discussed the architecture and working of colonial cities (fig. 37.20). The variety of small houses and the grand scale of the Governor's Palace inspired observations about class difference, slavery, and status. Students asked who cleaned all those windows, who built these buildings, and what kind of technology they had to build them.

Erin Riley

Erin is director of the Engineering and Design Lab at Greenwich Academy in Greenwich, Connecticut, United States, a preK–12 independent school for girls.

Marble run

Figure 37.21: Marble run.

I first used this Marble Machines project from the Exploratorium[1] on the fly with a camp using flexible tubing, molding, and pegboard (fig. 37.21).

The campers had a lot of fun, but the materials were really limited. Later we used it on a larger scale with the entire sixth grade as part of a Creativity Day event.[2]

Building with cardboard

Figure 37.22: Cardboard construction.

Cardboard is an excellent building material: flat and flexible yet strong—cheap, but can beautiful (fig. 37.22).

Machines that make machines

Figure 37.23: Materials cut for desktop milling machine.

An independent student summer project was to make the DIY Snap-Together CNC Milling Machine from the instructions from MIT's Machines That Make Machines project (figs. 37.23 and 37.24).[3]

Figure 37.24: Partially assembled desktop milling machine.

2D-design activities

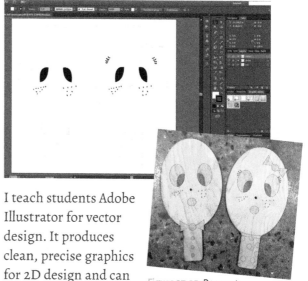

I teach students Adobe Illustrator for vector design. It produces clean, precise graphics for 2D design and can be used for outputting in the engineering lab.

Figure 37.25: Racquet paddles designed in Adobe Illustrator and cut on the CNC.

It is my favorite 2D design program for the laser cutter and CNC machines. Examples include iPod amps cut on the CNC (fig. 37.25) and cardboard keys cut on the laser (fig. 37.26).

Figure 37.26: Cardboard key designed in Adobe Illustrator and cut on the laser cutter.

Printmaking

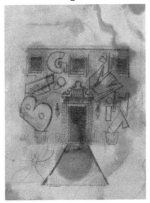

Figure 37.27: Laser-cut plate (wood).

Figure 37.28: Laser-cut plate (etching).

Printmaking can be a very controlled experience. I enjoy turning it around by introducing messy, unpredictable, painterly elements into the mix. Chine colle, splashy watercolor, and off-registration not only create beautiful objects but also encourage creative thinking. This year we used the laser cutter to create plates of wood (fig. 37.27) and etchings (fig. 37.28).

Drawing from observation

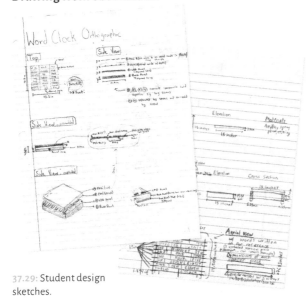

37.29: Student design sketches.

The visual recording of ideas is invaluable in making. Problems can be solved before an idea is built by hand or on the computer, or output to a machine for fabrication. Drawing helps us become better at observing and understanding the structure of the three-dimensional world. Architectural drawing with both isometric and linear perspectives (fig. 37.29) provides artists, designers, and engineers a language for describing ideas and plans. (See also chapter 23.)

Paper circuits

Figure 37.30: Beautiful paper circuit on marbled paper.

Enhancing paper engineering, pop-ups, and 2D design by introducing paper circuits with switches and LEDs adds a magical quality to the work (fig. 37.30).[4]

Sketchbooks/book binding

Bookmaking can be incorporated into all disciplines and can be customized for all subjects. It might be a sketchbook in art class, journal in English, or maker's lab book in the engineering lab. I also introduce papermaking,

Figure 37.31: Handmade sketchbooks..

marbling, and paste paper into book making; it's a bit of science and art and definitely magic. When students bind their own books, collect special materials (fig. 37.31), and even make their own paper (fig. 37.32), the investment is huge, and they pour their heart and soul into the pages.

Figure 37.32: Student-made paper.

Arduino mind map

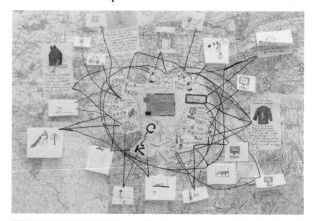

Figure 37.33: Arduino future project mind maps.

Our Engineering and Design class spent a couple of weeks working through all the projects found in an Arduino Starter Kit. The culminating project was a mind map—a brainstorming art project showing how these projects might be a springboard for new ideas (fig. 37.33). We hope some of these become future maker projects!

Atari punk synthesizer

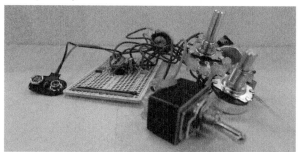

Figure 37.34: Circuit prototyping for synthesizer.

This project (figs. 37.34 and 37.35)[5] was designed for a circuits unit of an upper-school Engineering and Design elective.

Figure 37.35: Completed synthesizers.

Notes

1. tinkering.exploratorium.edu/sites/default /files/Instructions/marble_machines.pdf
2. fablearn.stanford.edu/fellows /MeaningfulMaking/CreativityDay.pdf
3. mtm.cba.mit.edu/machines/mtm_snap-lock
4. http://highlowtech.org/?p=2505
5. fablearn.stanford.edu/fellows /MeaningfulMaking/AtariPunkSynth.pdf

Tracy Rudzitis

Tracy established the makerspace and teaches computer applications and STEAM classes at M.S. 245, also known as The Computer School, a public grade 6–8 school in New York City, New York, United States.

3D-printed characters and props for stop-motion animation

Figure 37.36: 3D printed characters and props for stop-motion animation.

Sixth- and seventh-grade classes worked on stop-motion animation as part of the larger animation unit. The students came up with some brilliant and creative ideas using the 3D printer (fig. 37.36).

They had to work with scale and measurements to get the props to fit with the nonprinted items they were using. Prior to using the 3D printer, the students designed, drew, and painted the backdrops and scenery. With 3D printing, the students created three-dimensional objects, which opened up a new range of possibilities for what they could do with the tools and technologies available to them.

Very simple circuit

This was a hands-on workshop in circuits with a special education class. The students were thrilled to get some making experience. Although the activity is simple, the learning and understanding is not; none of these students knew about negative and positive or electricity and how it works, so it was all so magical to them.

Figure 37.37: It works!

We used copper tape, an LED, a battery, and paper (fig. 37.37). After we built paper circuits,

I hooked up a MaKey MaKey and was able to demonstrate how we can use our bodies (holding hands) to conduct electricity.[1]

Jitterbugs

The jitterbug is an excellent project for beginners or for when you may not have a lot of time to help out. This simple build uses recycled materials and a motor to make a robot.

Figure 37.38: Jitterbug—the random recycled robot.

Adding an off-center motor creates random jittering motion (fig. 37.38). There are many variations of this build found online,[2] and kits with preselected parts, but it's more fun and creative to not follow an explicit set of instructions and use parts one has on hand.

Materials

- Small DC motors
- Hook-up wire
- CD-ROMs (or other material for the robot body)
- Arts-and-crafts materials to decorate
- AA batteries
- Battery holders (optional)
- Masking tape

In the simplest build, these robots can be built using tape to hold the circuit together, secure the motor to the body, then decorate. To add more complexity and teach some useful skills, you can use this project to teach soldering to kids or have them teach it to each other. You can also 3D print the parts or the entire robot. There are kits available, but it's more fun to be creative and make your own.

Make something happen

This project was an end-of-the-year activity for sixth graders, most of whom had not had any making experience. We had forty-five minutes. I had the thirty-four students in each class sit at four tables with a basket with construction paper, markers, various lengths of hook-up wire, wire, pipe cleaners, alligator clips, assorted LEDs, coin cell batteries, and AA battery packs (the plastic ones with a negative and a positive wire coming from the terminals).

They played around with the materials in response to an open-ended challenge, "make something happen," and built a variety of objects (fig. 37.39). After thirty minutes I asked them questions like *What did you notice about the LEDs?*, *Were you able to make the lights light up?*, *Why?*, *Why not?* I asked them to look at what the others at the table were doing, and to notice how the coin cell battery was able to light up an LED. Although some of the students were already makerspace students, for many it was the first time in their life they had touched something electrical like that!

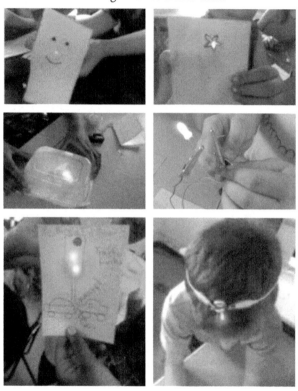

Figure 37.39: Building simple light-up circuits.

Notes

1. vimeo.com/96956333
2. exploratorium.edu/afterschool/activities /docs/jitterbug.pdf

Mark Schreiber

Mark is the director of design and innovation at The American School in Japan in Tokyo, Japan, an independent preK–12 school.

Squishy circuits with Arduino

I love making circuits with Squishy Circuit Dough,[1] and so do the kids. They get to explore how a circuit can work and how it can short out. But that's not all you can do with it. Once they learn the basics, we hook them up to small Arduinos (usually Adafruit's Gemma), then add a simple blink code that the students can tweak and change things like how fast it fades or how long it stays on and off.

Aerial photography

Figure 37.40: Arial photograph from weather balloon.

Aerial photography using cameras sent aloft with a weather balloon is a great activity (fig. 37.40). It costs a bit to have a helium tank, but if you do it right, you can reuse the weather balloon. It's nice to build a rig that can hold at least two cameras (if your balloon can lift that); then you can do two groups at a time.

It is a great design challenge for most age groups as the rig to hold a camera is pretty easy to design and create. Then I do a safety check on it, and away they fly. One idea to make it easier, faster, and get more rigs flying in less time might be to put the kite string on a modified bike rim. Then one can just crank in the balloon with the pedals and let it fly away with the freewheel.

I plan on doing the Global Space Balloon challenge[2] with my advanced class. It looks pretty cool. Basically you let the balloon/camera rig go up to burst altitude and then retrieve it using a GPS signal once it parachutes down. We will use an AdaFruit Arduino module or a Raspberry Pi USB device.

Monster scribble/art chalk bots

Scribble or art bots are one of my favorite tinkering activities. For older students or those who get bored with the small scribble bots (or toothbrush bots), challenge them with a larger bot. We use five-gallon buckets and cordless power tools to make monster chalk drawing bots.

Materials

- Sidewalk chalk
- Duct tape
- Cordless drill (with off-balance weight) or another power tool such as an orbital sander
- Five-gallon bucket or other big superstructure object
- A clean, fairly smooth sidewalk

Duct tape the sidewalk chalk to the upside-down bucket (legs) and secure the power tool to the top of the bucket. As the power tool vibrates, the monster chalk bot will randomly draw on the sidewalk.

Water/air rockets

Water rockets powered with compressed air have been around for a long time, but they continue to be a great activity for students. We use a two-liter pop bottle as the rocket body. For the fins foam core is easy to cut on the laser cutter for various designs. We pump them up to 90–100 psi using a rubber stopper, a PVC launcher, and a ball valve. If they are made correctly, they can easily go one hundred meters. We've also created payloads and parachutes, and we have coupled two bottles together for a longer "burn" with a Robinson coupling.[3]

6-3-5 upcycling designs

Upcycling is a low-cost way to get kids into design. I walk kids through the basic design thinking and iterative design cycle by having them come up with ideas based on a material, location, and activity. We use the Method 635,[4] a structured process to quickly generate multiple innovative ideas. Once the members of each student group settle on the idea, they have to rapidly prototype it. In other classes we refine the ideas using Method 635, give and get feedback, and then make a final prototype and "pitch" to the class. Whichever group's idea wins gets to do a small one-class production run of its idea.

We've created bike tube coffee cozies, wallets, bracelets, hair clips, utilitarian hooks, fire hose belts, guitar straps, and more.

IKEA hack-a-thon

Advanced classes do a hack-IKEA unit, where we use small objects (usually LED lamps and such) and repurpose them or combine them with other IKEA objects (typically kitchenwares). A maker camp activity for eight- to fourteen-year-olds involves hacking a nightlight, changing the LED with a different color, and replacing the lens with a student's laser-cut design for making shapes and patterns on ceilings.

Edible phone cases

Using rice crispy treats, we learn molding and casting techniques, vacuum bagging, and what makes a good design—then we eat the cases.

Shake it up

Have students create parts of a megametropolis city out of paper, foam core, etc., using Inkscape or Adobe Illustrator and the laser cutter. Once the city is assembled on a rocker platform (a piece of wood on rollerblade wheels with places to insert a jig saw to make it shake), turn on the "earthquake" and see how well the buildings hold up.

Open-source pinball

Figure 37.41: First step toward a pinball machine.

This is similar to a marble maze wall project but instead we made a pinball machine that can be easily reworked. It is basically a slanted pegboard, some bolts or dowels with rubber bands, a couple of flippers with push rods, and at the bottom a slanted rail that funnels the balls back to the shooter (rubber bands and PVC/rod or just PVC on a slope, as in figure 37.41). Kids enjoy tinkering with this.

Notes

1. courseweb.stthomas.edu/apthomas /SquishyCircuits/conductiveDough.htm
2. Global Space Balloon Challenge: youtu.be/iOyZoch_hb4
3. wrocket.hampson.net.au/?p=1081
4. wikipedia.org/wiki/6-3-5_Brainwriting

Aaron Vanderwerff

Aaron is the Creativity Lab director at Lighthouse Community Charter School, a public K–12 school in Oakland, California, United States.

CURRICULUM-INTEGRATED PROJECTS IN SUBJECT-AREA CLASSES

Mousetrap car (physics)

Figure 37.42: Building a mousetrap car.

In our high school physics class we ask students to build a mousetrap car at the beginning of our motion and forces unit (fig. 37.42). Students return from winter break with their prototype of a semifunctional car (which is supposed to move two inches at that point). From that point forward, we use students' cars to drive the curriculum; inevitably we talk about how we measure motion, mechanical advantage, and forces such as friction, gravity, and the elastic force of the springs. The difference is that students are the ones pushing us to study these topics so they can use physics to improve their designs. In addition, students isolate a single variable (such as wheel diameter or mass) and present their results to the class.

Building a mousetrap car is a time-honored tradition in high school physics, but by starting with the building of the car instead of using it as a capstone project, it gives a context for learning about motion and forces.

Wind turbine (physics)
Students in our physics class built their own wind turbines including winding their own coils for the generator. Using an initial design,[1] they then test

the output of the turbine and modify the wind turbine in some way to see if they can increase its output. Students modified the generator, turbine shape, turbine size, etc. Anecdotally, students understood power generation much better through this lesson than when using more traditional lessons.

TurtleArt: Introducing Cartesian coordinates (grades 5–6)

During this two-week-long miniunit,[2] students learned basic programming skills, deepened their understanding of angles, and were introduced to the Cartesian coordinates, all

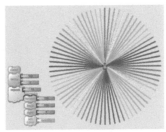

Figure 37. 43: Exploring Cartesian coordinates with TurtleArt.

using TurtleArt.[3] The first week, students learned to draw shapes and use the various blocks through investigation. During the second week, students made their favorite shape and then repeated that shape many times on their screen. This prompted students to explore a variety of blocks including the setxy block (fig. 37.43), which gave the class an opportunity to "discover" the Cartesian coordinate system that is built into TurtleArt.

Character study puppets (grade 2)

Figure 37.44: Puppet design.

In second grade, students study character traits of the main characters in folk tales and books they are reading. In this project, students sew puppets to represent these character traits using felt, thread, buttons, and found objects. They go through a simple design process to think about how they will represent the character trait they are trying to capture (fig. 37.44).

ELECTIVE AND ENRICHMENT PROJECTS

Chair (grades 7–12)

In high school, students complete a set of skill builders to learn skills they will have many opportunities to use in multiple projects. The first skill builder is to

Figure 37.45: Chair building teaches students to use power tools.

redesign and build a chair.[4] We provide students a sample from the previous year and ask them to improve the design. When students get to a step they don't know how to do (like using a circular saw), we coach them through it in groups of two to four (fig. 37.45).

Materials are all inexpensive (dimensional lumber and drywall screws), and our workspace consists of a few picnic benches outside. At the end of the project, students are comfortable drilling, sawing, and measuring, and the chairs are used for the rest of the year.

Sewing pillows (grades 5–12)

Similar to the chair skill builder, high school students sew pillows to learn to embroider, use a sewing machine, and create a plush object. Students start by embroidering a design on a piece of fabric (fig. 37.46), sew the side

Figure 37.46: Sewing is an essential skill in a makerspace.

of two squares of fabric together to make a pillow, and then stuff the pillow. The pillows are then used with the chairs.

Woodworking (kindergarten)

In the woodworking project, students learn to safely use tools and eventually design and build a toy for one of their classmates. The class starts by learning to sand and file; then students work with the teacher in small groups to learn to use a small hand saw (fig. 37.47). Skills such as using a hot glue gun, hammer, and drill are added to their repertoire throughout the quarter.

Kindergarteners build their tool literacy during the first quarter, which allows

Figure 37.47: Learning to use tools can start in kindergarten.

them to independently create projects throughout the year. Using what they have learned, students have built houses as tall as themselves, built a table for the class kitchen, and fixed toys.

Mini-makerspaces (grades 7–8)

Middle school elective students worked together to create classroom based mini-makerspaces[5] for a couple of our elementary classrooms using the design-thinking process. The students interviewed kindergarten teachers and observed the kindergarteners making. They then created designs for the mini-makerspaces and asked the students and teachers for feedback. Finally, using found objects (such as dressers), they built mini-makerspaces to help organize materials, tools, and projects.

Robot petting zoo (grades 7–12)

In collaboration with the TechHive[6] at the Lawrence Hall of Science, students built an interactive petting zoo.[7] The animals were built from cardboard using Hummingbird Robotics Kits[8] that are programmed using Scratch. Each animal has sensors (mostly motion, but some use sound) that allow the robots to react to a stimulus. When students "feed" the animals, they are actually triggering motion sensors, which then cause the animals to wiggle their ears or shout "Yum!"

Independent Maker Faire projects (grades 6–12)

The project with the longest track record is creating independent, student-driven projects that students showcase at the Bay Area Maker Faire, the largest Maker Faire in the world held every spring in San Mateo, California. First we lead students through a weeks-long ideation process. Then students come up with an idea for a project after completing some basic skill builders in the

fall. They create a prototype to share with the school community midway through the quarter and then display their project at Maker Faire.

Projects included a motion-sensitive LED tutu (fig. 37.48), a recycled plastic-bottle chandelier, a redwood bench for the schoolyard, and an electrical vehicle truck conversion.

Figure 37.48: A motion-sensitive light-up tutu that was exhibited at Maker Faire.

Notes

1. re-energy.ca/wind-turbine
2. TurtleArt lesson plans:
   fablearn.stanford.edu/fellows
   /MeaningfulMaking/TurtleArtProjectGuide.pdf
3. turtleart.org
   (free by e-mailing the authors of the software)
4. Chair building handout:
   fablearn.stanford.edu/fellows
   /MeaningfulMaking/ChairBuilding.pdf
5. lighthousecreativitylab.org/2015/06/2548
6. www.techhivestudio.org/makeathon
7. lighthousecreativitylab.org/2015/06
   /we-built-a-robot-petting-zoo
8. hummingbirdkit.com

Appendix
Project Snapshot Age or Grade Ranges, Materials + Supplies

The tables below provide recommended age or grade; tools, materials and supplies; and recommended software for the projects described in Project Snapshots. All ages and grades are approximate; accommodations can often be made for different ages. Use your own judgment to decide if these projects are appropriate for your own environment and participants. Refer to each project snapshot for more details.

Table A.1: Grade and age approximate equivalents

Level	Grade	Age
Lower elementary	K–3	Under 8
Upper elementary	3–6	8–10
Middle school	6–9	10–13
High school and beyond	9–12 (and up)	13 and up

Table A.2: Materials and supplies

This table lists examples of the types of materials and supplies used with the project snapshots in Tables A.3–A.5. See the snapshots for complete lists of materials. Makerspaces also provide students with appropriate tools such as scissors, cutters, and pliers, which are not listed here.

Materials and Supplies	Examples
Conductive fabrication	LEDs, copper tape, conductive thread, conductive yarn, conductive fabric, batteries, battery holders
Sewing	Fabric, felt, needles, snaps, buttons, sewing supplies
Craft	Tape, glue, scissors, clips, decorations, cardboard, paper, recycled materials
Electronics	Resistors, small motors, capacitors, breadboard, wire, potentiometers, buttons, switches
Building	Wood, metal, PVC pipe, nuts, bolts, screws

Table A.3: Community organizations

Project title	Approximate Grade				Tools	Materials/ Supplies	Software
	Lower Elementary	Upper Elementary	Middle School	High School + Beyond			
Susan Klimczak							
Flappy Bird game making with Scratch		X	X				Scratch
Musical Scratch		X					Scratch
Wooden cell phone holders			X	X		Wood, acrylic	Inkscape, LibreDraw
MaKey MaKey game controllers		X	X	X	MaKey MaKey	Conductive, craft	Scratch
MaKey MaKey conductivity game		X	X	X	MaKey MaKey	Conductive, craft	
Squishy circuit activities	X	X	X		Squishy circuit dough	Conductive, craft	
Machines Gone Wild!: Physical programming with cam mechanisms			X	X	Arduino, MotoProto Shield	Electronics, craft	Modkit Micro
Paper electronic storytelling		X	X	X	Circuit Stickers Kit	Conductive, craft	
No-sew electric friends		X	X	X		Sewing, conductive, craft	
RoboPicasso: Physical programming with VEX Robotics			X	X	VEX Robotics or LEGO motors	Pens	Modkit Micro
Chain-reaction machines with WeDo and Scratch: Physical programming	X	X	X		LEGO WeDo	Craft	Scratch
Starter project templates for Scratch game making	X	X	X				Scratch
Soft circuit pins and wearables		X	X	X	Laser cutter	Conductive fabrication, sewing, craft	

Table A.3: Community organizations (continued)

Project title	Approximate Grade				Tools	Materials/ Supplies	Software
	Lower Elementary	Upper Elementary	Middle School	High School + Beyond			
Susanna Tesconi							
Hidden sound: Experimenting with piezos, vibration, and amplifiers			X	X		Electronic, craft	
Playing with light: Lamp design				X	Laser cutter	Craft, electronics	Inkscape or Adobe Illustrator
Candy monsters			X	X	Miller, 3D printer		Tinkercad
Light gloves and light fingers		X	X	X		Sewing, conductive fab	
Teacher training: No-battery lab						Craft, building	
Teacher training: Montessori-inspired material					Laser cutter	Craft, building	
Make it big: Scaled-up Scrabble-type game			X	X	Laser cutter	Building	
What do elderly people need?			X	X			
Nalin Tutiyaphuengprasert							
Parents' maker day	X	X	X	X	Laser cutter		Adobe Illustrator
Videoconference to showcase students' ideas		X	X	X			
Fab Lab in your class							
Minisculpture	X					Craft	
Box maker	X	X			Laser cutter	Craft	
Design your house	X				Laser cutter		Adobe Illustrator
Pop-pop boat competition		X	X			Craft	
Elevation drawing		X	X		Calipers	Craft	
Mother's Day pop-up card with basic electronic circuits	X	X				Conductive fabrication	

Table A.3: Community organizations (continued)

Project title	Approximate Grade				Tools	Materials/ Supplies	Software
	Lower Elementary	Upper Elementary	Middle School	High School + Beyond			
Juliet Wanyiri							
Redesigning our cities	X	X	X	X	Laser cutter	Electronics, conductive fabrication, craft, building	
Video games and virtual worlds: Programming with Scratch		X	X				Scratch
Intelligent house and car		X	X	X	LEGO bricks and kits	Electronics, craft	
Building a bike-powered smoothie maker (bici-blender)				X		Pedal-powered machinery, building, electronics	
3D printing meets paper electronics	X	X			3D printer	Conductive fabrication	
The clapping car: An introduction to sensors	X	X			Picocricket kit		
Electronic quiz board		X	X		Picocricket kit	Craft	
Simple origami lights	X	X	X			Conductive fabrication	

Table A.4: Museums

Project title	Approximate Grade				Tools	Materials/ Supplies	Software
	Lower Elementary	Upper Elementary	Middle School	High School + Beyond			
Keith Ostfeld							
Cardboard automata		X	X	X		Craft	
Light painting		X	X		Digital camera	Conductive fabrication	
Zoetrope		X	X			Craft	
Duct tape making		X	X			Duct tape	
Top making		X	X			Craft	
LED bling	X	X	X	X		Conductive fabrication	

Table A.5: Schools

Project title	Approximate Grade				Tools	Materials/ Supplies	Software
	Lower Elementary	Upper Elementary	Middle School	High School + Beyond			
Jaymes Dec							
Make something that makes art		X	X	X			
Interactive dioramas		X	X	X			
Nerdy Derby		X	X	X		Building	
High-contrast portraiture			X	X	Vinyl cutter		
MaKey MaKey instrument		X	X	X	MaKey MaKey	Conductive, craft	
Light-up bracelet		X	X	X		Conductive fabrication, conductive, sewing	
Make your space a better place	X	X	X	X			
Environmental concern				X			
Project ideas from Constructing Modern Knowledge 2014							
Gilson Domingues							
Little Thomas Edisons: Assembling and inventing			X	X	Gogo Board, Gogo Mini	Electronics, craft	
Little Turings: Programming robots and other devices			X	X	Gogo Board, Gogo Mini, Arduino, laser cutter	Electronics	

Table A.5: Schools (continued)

Project title	Approximate Grade				Tools	Materials/ Supplies	Software
	Lower Elementary	Upper Elementary	Middle School	High School + Beyond			
David Malpica							
Engineering design intersession			X				
Design the School of the Future competition			X				
Redesign of 3D-printed Robohands		X			3D printer, calipers		Tinkercad
Laser-cut habitat animals and mythological creatures		X			Laser cutter		Meshmixer
3D gnomes skill builder	X	X					Autodesk 123D Design or Tinkercad
Kinetic sculptures			X			Craft	
Turtle racing game		X	X				Scratch and PencilCode or TurtleArt
Costa Rica eco-tourism experience			X		Laser cutter	Craft	123D Design and 123D Make
Heather Allen Pang							
National History Day exhibit boards			X	X			
Advisory project modified for laser cutter			X	X	Laser cutter	Craft	
Lined bag: Introduction to sewing by machine			X	X	Sewing machine	Sewing	
Skill builder: Inkscape buildings			X	X	Laser cutter	Inkscape	

Table A.5: Schools (continued)

Project title	Approximate Grade				Tools	Materials/ Supplies	Software
	Lower Elementary	Upper Elementary	Middle School	High School + Beyond			
Erin Riley							
Marble run	X	X	X	X		Tubing, pegboard	
Building with cardboard	X	X	X	X		Cardboard, craft	
Machines that make machines			X	X	Laser cutter		
2D-design activities			X	X	Laser cutter, CNC machine		Adobe Illustrator
Printmaking			X	X			
Drawing from observation			X	X			
Paper circuits		X	X	X		Conductive fabrication, craft	
Sketchbooks/book binding			X	X			
Arduino mind map				X			
Atari punk synthesizer				X		Electronics, building	
Tracy Rudzitis							
3D-printed characters and props for stop-motion animation		X	X	X	3D printer, camera		
Very simple circuit	X	X	X			Conductive fabrication, craft, electronics	
Jitterbugs	X	X	X			Electronics, craft	
Make something happen	X	X	X			Electronics, craft	

Table A.5: Schools (continued)

Project title	Approximate Grade				Tools	Materials/ Supplies	Software
	Lower Elementary	Upper Elementary	Middle School	High School + Beyond			
Mark Schreiber							
Squishy circuits with Ardunio			X	X	Squishy circuit dough, Gemma	Conductive fabrication supplies	
Aerial photography			X	X	Camera, GPS-enabled Arduino or Raspberry Pi, balloon	Electronic	
Monster scribble/ art chalk bots			X	X	Power tools	Craft	
Water/air rockets			X	X		Craft	
6-3-5 upcycling designs	X	X	X	X		Craft	
IKEA hack-a-thon			X	X		Craft, building	
Edible phone cases			X		Rice Krispy treats	Craft	
Shake it up			X	X	Laser cutter	Craft	Inkscape or Adobe Illustrator
Open-source pinball			X	X		Craft, building	
Aaron Vanderwerff							
Mousetrap car				X		Building	
Wind turbine						Electronics, craft, building	
TurtleArt: Introducing Cartesian coordinates		X	X				TurtleArt
Character study puppets	X					Craft, sewing	
Chair			X	X		Building	
Sewing pillows		X	X	X		Craft, sewing	
Woodworking	X					Building	
Mini-makerspaces			X				
Robot petting zoo			X	X	Hummingbird Robotics Kits		Scratch
Independent Maker Faire projects			X	X			

CPSIA information can be obtained
at www.ICGtesting.com
Printed in the USA
FSOW03n1326020616
21017FS